The Ultimate Step By Step Guide To Finding & Investing In Off-Market Real Estate:

How I Turned $39,000 Into $50 Million In Nine Years By Finding And Unlocking Hidden Equity Before Anyone Else

Dedication

To my family: I really do love you more than my computer!

I see them rolling their eyes, but I don't even know where to begin thanking everyone who made this all possible.

I guess we should start with Shoshi Koren, my biggest fan since she was changing my diapers. Mom, I know you thought I never noticed, but your bottomless support and unbreakable spirit kept me going through even the worst of times. My dreams would have stayed fantasy if it wasn't for your generous and ever-present kind soul waving me to the top of every mountain.

But even that endless encouragement wouldn't have been enough without dad keeping me grounded and focused. I know I resisted your teachings at the time, but you made me the man I am today. Lord knows, you sure drilled in me the passion to work with my mind instead of my hands!

Then there's Max. My partner, mentor and brother from another mother. The first multi-tasking workaholic I ever met that put me to shame, and made it look easy. Seems like just yesterday we were shotgunning crazy business plans off of one another over lunch, each trying to top the other. Who could have imagined back then what we have accomplished? You made life a richer experience and I'm forever in your debt for taking this wild-eyed computer nerd under your wing.

And there are so many others, but so little space here!

Orna Eizenman - My High School Teacher

It's the rare teacher that can teach a child that rarely even showed up to reach for the stars! You're the one destined for bigger things.

Gil Perlberg - My commanding officer in the IDF

Thank you so much for believing in some rebellious soldier and giving me the confidence to believe in myself in the harshest circumstances. You pulled my butt from the fire and put me back on the road to success.

To my mates Ryan Taylor and James Weley from London – You know what I'm thankful for. I'll owe you both forever for getting my foot in the door.

And Avi Yahav, don't think I forgot about you. I wouldn't even be here in America without the plentiful help of the kindest good Samaritan I ever met. When I had no place to turn to, you were there. Thank you.

Caridad Morales – My sweet, endlessly patient cleaning madam that has added years to my life by saving all the time I'd otherwise waste living like a grown-up!

And to the hundreds of others receiving a free copy of this book, I'm sorry there isn't space to list you all here, but you're never far from my heart.

Now enough of the sappy stuff before I cry. Let's make some money!

Table of Contents

Pre-Purchase Checklist: Will this book add value for me?

- Are you a stock market investor tired of being at the mercy of high-speed trading algorithms and random headline news events? Do you ever wish you had more control over your investments? Have you avoided direct real estate investment because you weren't quite sure how to leverage big data to buy off-market properties at +90% discounts, with a minimum of 30% equity?

- Are you a real estate professional trying to bring more value to your clients and really stand out from the pack? Would you like to take your skillset to a whole new level and earn 10x the commissions with half the work?

- Are you a current investor frustrated about all the competition nowadays and the ever-thinning margins? Would you like to skip the direct mailing campaigns and generate vetted leads before anyone else?

Don't forget to check out the free hour-long companion video to this book. Since it's so much easier to show, rather than tell, I put together a big picture video overview that covers everything you're reading here, from A-Z, on some real-world examples.

Real estate is all about building relationships, which is why I love nothing more than chatting all day. Please shoot me any questions, concerns or random thoughts you have and I'll respond as fast as possible.

www.lirankoren.com

www.luxurypropertycare.com

Who Am I To Lecture Anyone?

"Try not to become a man of success. Rather become a man of value."

– Albert Einstein

Oh, I was sweating rivets all right, but for once it had nothing to do with the boiling South Florida humidity. The straining air conditioner did nothing to tamp down the heated greed radiating from the 50 filthy rich investors wedged into a small conference room built for 20 in the courthouse. This was a whole new type of pressure cooker. A melting reactor core of runaway high-octane American capitalism.

This was a foreclosure auction in the middle of the Great Housing Crash in early 2009. My very first auction ever.

In Broward County, Florida of all places. Ground zero of some of the worst real estate slaughter in modern history. And all the sharks were circling. You had local big shots I recognized from their TV commercials, out of state real estate moguls with multiple suitcases bulging with cash, bodyguards, pro real estate agents talking on several phones at once, even bargain hunting personal shoppers looking to gobble up a few more vacation homes for their Saudi Arabian royalty clients.

And then there was me.

Shuffling from foot to foot in the middle of the pack, I did my best to look like a big boy who knew what he was doing. One of the court security officers kept frowning at me like he was wondering where my parents were. I was so confident I had everything in grip, at least back when my partner and I had this hare-brained scheme to "get rich" at the next property auction. It was going to be so easy, right?

Sure, I'd dabbled in a couple of on-market real estate purchases and had nearly my entire life savings tied up in a pair of rental condominiums. I fancied myself a savvy investor, but it hit me all at once how far above my weight class I was swinging. I was a recent

1

immigrant and boring nerd. My specialty was fixing computer networking issues, not playing real-life Monopoly.

I didn't have the money to burn, connections to get insider information or even the slightest formal training on real estate. Just an old laptop full of some Excel spreadsheets and who knew if they were even accurate estimates about equity in different auction items. All I knew about property auctions was what I read the night before on Wikipedia and the court's website. What chance did I have?

I'll be honest, the flight or fight response kicked in when I glanced at the walk clock. Two minutes until it all began. I could turn and walk away right now without losing a thing.

Except for my pride. Thankfully, like always, I was too arrogantly stubborn to give up.

So I counted to ten and ground my teeth, rolling my shoulders to warm up for whatever was in store. I'd served three years in the Israeli Self Defense Forces. I burnt all the midnight oil working 100-hour weeks managing IT services for major London banks. Then put in eight-day workweeks building my own computer services firm from scratch when I immigrated to America with nothing but the clothes on my back and a few months of savings. All before I turned 27. Stress was my mistress. Adrenaline my muse. Conquering an "impossible" challenge the only reason worth getting out of bed in the morning.

"You got this! You've always worked harder and smarter than any of these rich old fools!"

Some older man pressing against my shoulder in the crowd kept muttering a similar motivational pep talk over and over. I turned and shot him a sympathetic wink...only he just squinted at me and puckered his lips.

Was I mumbling out loud?

I tried to laugh it off. "Sorry, just a touch of nerves. I wasn't talking about you."

He shook his leather satchel, bulging with reams of printouts, at the laptop I clutched tight to my chest.

"This your first time, son? You worried you're in over your head?"

I snorted but my mouth went dry and tripped up my words. A flicker of a smile danced across his leathery face.

"Good, because that's how you learn to swim."

He shrugged and yawned. "Or at least make room for the rest of us."

Bang

Like a starter pistol, the court clerk tapped his gavel down as the clock struck 10:00. The milling herd sprang to attention while some Bank of America rep stood up and barked:

"Case number 10-45734, going for $90,000…"

That was all the information they gave back then, and not much has changed today. Just a lawsuit number and the mortgage holder's opening bid. What type of property? What's the address? That was your problem to find out. If you weren't obsessively tracking the court's public records before the auction, you were out of luck. In this frenzied game, taking just ten seconds to see if topping the latest bid still makes this a good deal for you was enough to lose out.

Clearly though, some people had done their homework. Or at least a little bit. A man and a woman shouted "$95,000!" at the same time and snarled at each other. Some other guy sped read through his computer. I could count every kilobyte of data he painstakingly downloaded on the overloaded local Wi-Fi by the pace of his stomping foot.

"Uh, $100,000!"

Someone else covered one ear and pressed a phone to the other. "Are you sure? Does the MLS match up?" Two seconds later, he screamed around his phone at the auctioneer. "$105 g's!"

All the other bidders shrugged and stayed quiet. The man with the slow internet connection bit his lip and flipped a coin. He just shook his head when the bank rep raised an eyebrow his way.

"3, 2, 1… sold. Next case number 10-757120, going for $50,000…"

3

The whole process took less than 60 seconds.

I couldn't help but whistle. I mean, I knew intellectually that the county had around four hundred properties to auction off in just seven hours, so things must move fast. But to actually witness six figure deals closing in only one or two minutes was mind blowing. And these people did this every single day! What had I gotten myself into?

I steadied my nerves by opening up my laptop and squeezing into a few inches of space at the nearest table. Maybe I didn't understand all the terminology these big players were tossing around, and I sure didn't have millions in play money to gamble away on speculative investments, but I had two aces up my sleeve.

The first was that beautiful Excel spreadsheet glowing in my face, matching each case number to the corresponding property and listing every scrap of publicly available data on each item in the day's auction. Maybe it was an overkill, since I only had the money to bid on one, maybe two places if the prices were really good... but now I could pluck the best deals out of a river of foreclosures and ignore the rest. It struck me then that my real vulnerability wasn't naivety. Quite the contrary.

I knew too much.

"You must have a much better internet connection than I do. Are you using an air card or something..."

I gulped when some real estate agent next to me at the packed table started to peer around at my screen. Without a word, I snatched up my gear and scurried to a corner of the room.

Squatting down against the wall, I wrapped the computer against my chest like a newborn baby. Sure, I had a polarizer lens on the screen to keep curious eyes away, but I still kept adjusting the angle of my screen every time someone moved around me. These big shot investors were rich enough. I wasn't ready to share my gold mine of custom designed webscrapers. The boring data on my computer was worth far more than the envelope full of cash in my pocket.

I had my scripts running all through the previous night, pulling and cross-referencing records from the property appraiser's, tax assessor's and clerk of court's websites, plus the MLS listings and CoreLogic comps. Then I spent most of the morning filtering the leads to ignore anything with less than 30% equity and applying my own valuation process to the best deals.

If that sounds melodramatic, remember these were the dark, dog-eat-dog days of 2009, when the "sky was falling" across the real estate world. Or raining mana from heaven, depending on how much data you had on hand. And I can't stress enough how powerful information was and still is in this business. The slightest little bit of trivia on a property can make the difference between a killer investment or going underwater like the previous homeowner. The constant cries of frustration in the crowded room every time a website buffered and someone had to guess at a bid was proof enough.

Still, I had another ace in the hole. My partner, Max Hefter, strutted in five minutes after the auction started, after at least six deals were closed. The ol' construction foreman and founder of his own successful textile supply business glided towards me through the sea of shouting, cussing millionaires like he owned the place.

"Why you kneelin' in the corner, Liran? Are you in time out?"

He plopped down a couple of foldable campstools. They even had cup holders for the fresh coffee he brought along. Like always, Max had every little detail planned out ahead of time.

I tried to match his monk-like calm, but my voice squeaked out of my pounding chest. "They just changed bank reps. I think the cases we wanted are coming up next. Did you get it?"

Max tossed me a thumb drive. My shaky hands managed to plug it in on the third try.

"Yep, I called up every bank lawyer on our hot list and just asked them pointblank what their price is. No time to check out the houses in person, but we now know every opening bid they're going to place ahead of time. So what's the new equity tally?"

Buying cheap properties at auction might seem like an easy game. A classic case of buy low, sell high. Lenders prefer to hold onto stacks of paper debt that they can resell multiple times through "financial engineering" schemes. Since the last thing in the world a bank wants is to keep a physical inventory of properties that costs them money, they would discount their opening bid and dump every foreclosure fast, often accepting just pennies on the dollar. They're only marginally less risk adverse nowadays. It's all a bargain hunter's dream, if you knew what the bank's opening bid was before the auction began and didn't have to waste precious seconds running a new equity estimate.

Which I now knew, thanks to Max.

While everyone else scrambled to look up equity and value in those fleeting moments after the banker read the case and bid off, Max and I already knew if the property was worth bidding on. And exactly how high we could go and still guarantee a comfortable profit. While they shouted bids against each other in the frantic heat of the moment, we could take our time and think about every dollar we were risking. Time to bid calmly and confidently might sound like a small advantage, but it made all the difference back then and still does today.

For a brief minute, the local wi-fi went down just then. Not that it was a problem for us. I had everything offline and hadn't even bothered to connect to the internet. While the rest of my more experienced peers screamed into phones and cussed at the air, it took me just a few clicks to update my entire spreadsheet and sort out the new hot leads. We skipped the next few properties, since I could see right off the bat that the profit margins were too slim, but then we finally had a case that was on my shortlist.

"There it is, Max. It's got a $90,000 spread between the bank's bid and the value. We can't spend more than—"

"… going for $15,000."

And we were off to the races.

"Twenty!" "Thirty!" "Thirty-five!"

I hadn't even opened my mouth yet and we were near the edge of what I calculated our max offer should be. Most of the room dropped out of the bidding fast.

The last man standing was actually sitting, as relaxed and in control in his Armani suit as if it were his bathrobe. The guy hogging up one of the few tables in the room wasn't an agent, and sure as heck wasn't an amateur investor like me. I never learned his name, but it was clear he was the big-shot money man behind the scenes. The no-nonsense bodyguard perched behind him, with muscles hiding where his triceps ended and his neck began, gave that away. Hovering around Mr. Money Bags, a small army of real estate agents whispered into their phones while shoving noses into their computers.

"Thirty-six!" I blurted the number out at the top of my lungs, which apparently came out as a squeak. The bank rep cupped his ear my way.

"What was that, sir?"

Mr. Money Bags tilted his head, giving me a once over from my scoffed loafers to the top of my cheap off-the-rack suit. He turned up his nose and snapped his fingers at one of his agents. If they were running the same type of calculations as me, I knew what that team was going to bid next. So I cut them off and jumped a bit ahead of them.

"I said thirty-eight thousand!"

Money Bags rolled his eyes and muttered at his agent. She barked out "Forty!" before crossing her arms and staring me down.

Max elbowed me as I opened my mouth. He leaned in to check my screen, but I knew what he was going to say. My spreadsheet put our max bid at $39,000, so we should be out of the running... but how could I be sure I hadn't made a mistake? What if I was too conservative in my home valuation? A few percentage points shouldn't make a difference, right?

As usual, Max cut straight through the fog.

"Hold up. Is this really such a good deal? What's a three-bedroom house in that cookie-cutter neighborhood doing without an attached garage?" He reached over and clicked on the home photos I had downloaded.

"Ah, you see that? They converted the garage into a new den, but that's not reported on the property appraiser's site. We're looking at some big code enforcement fines and inspection fees. Likely they used a cheap contractor too, from what I see in the uneven façade work, so that'll need to be fixed. Call it at least five grand to get everything squared away. God knows what other surprises are inside if the owners cut so many corners."

"… and sold. Next case…"

While Max and I high-fived over the close call, Mr. Money Bags grinned and delved into his bulging briefcase. He pulled out the 5% deposit in hard cash and sauntered over to the cashier's window. Seconds after he paid the clerk, one of his agents hung up with what I guessed was another rep in the field surveying the new purchases. The rich investor shook his head and laughed when he heard the bad news about his new investment. I gritted my teeth and stayed focused on the next hot case coming up. Maybe it was a game for him, but Max and I didn't have money to burn. There was no room for error.

Which thankfully, wasn't a great concern for us. No, we didn't have unlimited resources nor assistants, but we still stacked the deck in our favor by harvesting plenty of publicly available data, which I'll show you exactly how to do as well.

We kept at it the rest of the morning, cross referencing each new case number with our data to see instantly whether there was equity in the home, and if so, exactly how much we could bid and still have a safe margin of error in this free-falling market.

We passed on several more cases and were outbid on a couple. In the downtime, Max looked over my work and offered his own insights. He pointed to one in particular that was halfway down my list.

"Why isn't this condo at the top of the pile? I know that neighborhood. High quality, next to the university, plenty of rental opportunities. Probably the only area in town where the home prices are sort of stable. I know you're obsessed with equity, but isn't how fast we can resell a place just as important? So I think you actually undervalued it a bit here."

I did a quick manual recalculation and he was right. Unlike most of the other properties, its comps weren't dominated by foreclosures. A single foreclosure was driving down the comp average, and that was for an apartment two blocks away. Once I replaced the outlier with a better fit condo from the same building and hit "filter by largest value" in Excel, sure enough, this property jumped all the way to the top of the equity column.

Built and sold two years previously for $230k, the final judgment was about $260k. With the old comp's saying the market value was only $52,000, the bank would open with a $39,300 bid. Anyone using an automated comp program, like say auction bidders with only 60 seconds to manually figure out a home's value, would still have that old market estimate of $52k. So this property wasn't exactly a great deal if you're following the 70/30 rule.

But with a quick manual comp search, the real value was at least $90,000.

Could we really be the only ones to notice that? Max and I whistled at the same time when the case was called shortly before lunch. I started to shout "$40,000," fully expecting someone else to figure out the property's value and to run up the price in short order, but the sudden quiet in the room as everyone scurried to look up the incredibly discounted condo gave me an idea.

Instead of whooping and hollering, I just yawned and mentioned "39,400" before anyone placed a bid.

The next ten seconds of complete silence were the longest of my life. Without the fevered call to arms from an excited investor signaling that a place was particularly interesting, it was difficult for the other bidders to muster the motivation to mess with yet another hasty property evaluation on something so "low value." Afterall, it was a fatiguing process. Every single minute a new scramble to be the first to learn just what an investment is worth, and then repeat that nonstop for hours.

Only Mr. Money Bag's team of agents seemed busy. At the last second, one of his people leaned back and whispered something in the big man's ear. The boss cocked his brow briefly, then glanced over at us. Max's calm must have rubbed off on me, because I managed to keep my foot from tapping too fast and somehow got my fidgeting hands to stay still.

Money Bag's grunted. "If the comps were really wrong, that guy would have noticed. Don't worry about this one. We have bigger fish to catch."

"Going in 3, 2, 1... Sold!"

It was the most beautiful and scary thing I'd ever seen. No one bid against us.

Did we just pull a coup or screwed ourselves over?

Max and I didn't say a word as we stood and marched over to the cashier's counter. My trembling hands dropped a few bills as I tugged an envelope from my pocket and pried out my half of the cash deposit. The cashier gave us a receipt and that was that.

Now the clock was ticking. We had until noon the next day to pay the remaining 95% or abandon our deposit. I'm sure the court considered this a "cool down" period to reconsider the deal, but my mind was racing even faster than before.

Max clapped my back. "That was fun. What do you say we go do a drive-by and actually see what we just bought?"

"You do that. You know what we're looking for. I'm going to the lawyer's office and hover over his shoulder while he does the title search."

Twelve tense days later, after running multiple title searches and badgering my attorney with a million questions, we finally took full title.

We drove straight from the attorney's office to the condo, meeting a couple of Max's contractors at the door. We were ready for anything when we unlocked the door, except for what we found.

The place was immaculate. 100% move-in ready. The last occupant had even vacuumed right before moving out.

Instead of flipping fast, we wound up renting it out at premium rates for a few years before finally cashing out at $170,000.

But it's more than just the wealth. I can't describe how it feels to buy your first property blind at auction and then see the actual asset...

There aren't words, but one thing was clear. Since that day, Max and I had a new career. We knew exactly where we wanted to spend our time and money!

I abandoned my computer services company and dived all into real estate. Not just foreclosure auctions, but pre-foreclosure deals directly with homeowners, tax auctions, short sales—you name it. It wasn't just a way to make money, a hobby or even an ego thing. Off-market real estate was an addiction. The challenge and the thrill of hunting and negotiating for hidden equity is just something you can't find in most industries. I read every book on the subject I could find and followed countless court cases and title transfers, just to see how things worked out. I took note of the most equity-rich deals and interrogated every investor, real estate attorney and listing agent involved until even they got bored talking shop.

But it paid off. Max and I sure didn't have deep pockets, and we never took on another partner. We never needed to. There are other, even more valuable forms of capital than money.

If you invest in yourself and bring new skills to the business, you will dominate your field, no matter how much cash you start with. Because the money will come eventually to anyone focused on what value they can add to an enterprise, rather than just how they can make a quick buck.

While that first deal back in 2009 might have been enough to land us a rich silent investor, Max and I decided to fund ourselves. With me hunting down equity before the competition and him handling the nuts and bolts of home rehab and staging, we ramped our inventory up to 20 units that first year. Despite the profits piling up, neither of us cashed out after the first few deals. Quite the opposite, we poured in every spare cent we could scavenge up during that first year. We rolled every dollar back into the company, even deferring taxes ad infinitum through 1031 exchanges.

We had agreed that we wouldn't allow ourselves a single penny in profit until we reached $1 million in revenue. I can't stress enough how critical this part is. Say you're starting with only $20,000 in capital. You make $10,000 in clear profit from your first deal after three months. Many investors will cash out a large chunk of that new business equity, only growing their "war chest" incrementally. But if you're adding value-capital yourself, you want exponential growth. So if you keep that $30k fund intact, you can now do two $15k deals at once, which should nearly double your funds in the second quarter. Then you can do four deals the next quarter and so on and so on.

That was the exact model we used. Oh, we held onto a few rental properties to keep up a steady cash flow, but mostly focused on bringing off-market homes to market as fast as possible. While none of our flips were particularly large, the compounding returns from the high volume were breathtaking. During that first year, our average total investment in each property came out to $50,000 in '09 dollars. That's counting everything from initial purchase to rehab, holding and closing costs. We only targeted properties with at least 30% equity, and netted an average profit on each home of only 20% after all expenses.

Not to say there weren't plenty of deals that yielded 50%-100%, what we called "candy" investments. More than enough to offset the occasional mistakes we made and still turn a hefty net profit. These sweet candy deals had nothing to do with luck. It's all about that boring old data advantage. What other investors call luck is just a statistical certainty when you're a persistent and well-informed buyer. When you can bid calmly at auction or make a firm offer directly to a homeowner, confidently and methodically on many properties a day, you'll pick up great deals. You'll have a vast edge when other people hesitate because they don't have ready info on the available equity or don't know the neighborhood.

The net result for the year was $1 million in revenue and $200,000 in pre-tax profit, all from an initial investment of $250,000 (pumped in slowly throughout the course of the year). And that was mostly from simple auction flips. It wasn't until later that we branched out and discovered the immense value of buying title directly from homeowners in the early pre-foreclosure period, or gaining title cheap through HOA auctions or any of the legal tricks that can drastically lower a lender's payoff amount.

Fast forward nine years after that modest beginning and we've now generated over $50 million in revenue from traditional property flipping alone, not counting bonus rental income and capital appreciation from several dozen "alternative" deals.

I don't mention this to brag, but to show how luck, connections or even deep pockets aren't necessary to kick ass in real estate investing. Granted, in a non-collapsing housing market like we have today, you'll definitely spend more on each deal than those crazy days in '09, but with higher property values across the board the equity ratio isn't any different. So there's no reason you can't surpass our returns. Especially since this book and my online courses will accelerate your learning process by many years and save you from making some extremely costly mistakes.

And to reiterate the core theme of this book: equity is the most important consideration when evaluating any investment. You might have bad luck with tenants or misjudged how cheap and fast you can flip a property, but if you're only dealing in properties with huge reserves of equity, you'll always come out "in the black" on any deal.

That simple principle is the number 1 secret to my success. When folks call me a "guru" now, I still don't believe it. Sometimes it feels like just yesterday that I was a recent immigrant. A computer geek with no real estate background. I couldn't even spell "Lis Pendens" at first, and my accent was so thick in the beginning that Max often needed to translate my English when talking with homeowners.

But I pulled it off to become the apex investor in my local market, so there's absolutely no reason you can't surpass that success as well.

The "secret formula to success in real estate" is actually quite simple: never be surprised, never be greedy and never stop learning.

We made plenty of mistakes along the way, that's true, but we were never taken by surprise at any point. We stuck to a methodical, data-driven approach that focused on equity, speed of return and cost effectiveness for every step of the process. Some were great deals earning us double our investment, some didn't sell as fast as we liked so we accepted sub-par offers that netted us as little as 5% profit.

The key to it all though was constant learning. When something went right, I obsessed over every legal, financial and personal detail to figure out how we can do even better next time. When things went sideways, I went into 10x the detail to learn how to ensure it never happens again.

That is the simple point of this book and my online courses: to drastically cut that learning curve down for you, saving you tens of thousands of dollars and years of stress in the process.

Ok, granted, maybe there's a large dose of ego indulgence tossed in the mix. Because at this point, the money is just a game. When you've already made millions in a particular field, a little more cash doesn't make that much of a difference. The one thing money can't buy though is the self-satisfaction I savor every time a client calls me up to invite me to their "New Millionaire Bash."

As I penned this book in 2018 and searched for a way to articulate just how much room there is at the top, I figured I'd simply let the numbers speak for themselves. Right now, the total value of real estate owned by private individuals in the United States is about $25.6 trillion, with total outstanding mortgages of $10.3 trillion.

So we're talking about $15.2 *trillion* in privately held home equity.[1]

It's a grand, all you can eat buffet. My dream is to make sure everyone gets a seat at the table.

---

[1] Board of Governors of the Federal Reserve System (U.S.), Households and Nonprofit Organizations; Home Mortgages; Liability, Level [HHMSDODNS], retrieved from FRED, Federal Reserve Bank of St. Louis; https://fred.stlouisfed.org/series/HHMSDODNS Dec. 18, 2018.

Busting The Most Common Myths And Misunderstandings Scaring Investors Away.

1) You need a ton of capital to get started.

This is by far the most damaging myth that makes so many investors miss out on this vast marketplace. There is nothing stopping you from building a multi-property real estate empire in one year, with a $1 million plus market value, using less capital than it takes to buy a new car. And I'm not talking about putting up a down payment to take out a loan or any such financial leverage. In fact, when you're just beginning, you should try to stay away from any sort of debt financing. Instead, use the techniques you learn here to leverage small amounts of your capital into controlling interest over an expensive property.

For example, with just $5,000 in initial cash, and sometimes even less depending on your local marketplace, you can position yourself to gain title through a Home Owner's Association (HOA) lien and even eliminate the original lender's interest in some states. At a minimum, you can easily outbid everyone when the place eventually goes to auction because of your surplus right's assignment. I'll cover all the details on how to pull this off in Phase Two.

If you have a little bit more cash, I'll show you how to find off-market, pre-foreclosure "distressed" properties before everyone else. Then you can go straight to the homeowner and take title to a $200,000 home for $10-20k. Add in a bit more to get the place up to selling standards, but the big ticket expenses like paying off the mortgage and other debt isn't your problem. The buyer you resell to will take care of that. You're leveraging *their* mortgage instead of your own to keep your capital outlays at a bare minimum.

2) Real estate is a speculative investment, just like the stock market, but without the ability to liquidate a bad investment fast.

Sure, there are many real estate investing niches and styles, and some of them are quite risky. The strategies I'm laying out here though don't involve any speculation. Luck, the general marketplace or whims of buyers don't play a role when you follow a data-driven, equity-focused approach to investing. Best of all, since this is all a numbers game rather than an art, I can teach anyone who is willing to invest a few hours of their time how to do this.

We're hunting existing equity, so we know we can sell our inventory at a guaranteed profit in a hurry. Essentially, we're looking for arbitrage-like opportunities, rather than just discounts. As long as you only invest in properties with plenty of equity, you will always be in low-risk positions and hold semi-liquid assets that will sell in short order at some level of profit.

Contrast that strategy to playing the stock market. On Wall Street, all equity is incredibly overpriced. Every penny of equity you can find is selling for a major multiplier over its value, even in a bear market. So is stock XYZ really a good buy at 20x it's P/E ratio, just because today it happened to trade below the 50-day moving average? You're still spending $20 to buy every $1 worth of equity, just in the hope that someone else is going to come after you and pay even more. You can point to all the technical indicators you want to justify that gamble, but at the end of the day it's still just speculation. You're completely at the mercy of the broader marketplace and don't have any edge over anyone else. Your only safety margin is how much you can tolerate losing while waiting impotently for the price to swing in your favor.

How about playing a different game? One where you set the rules. Instead of spending $50,000 to purchase a $2,500 stock equity stake and gamble that the price will go up soon, why not just buy guaranteed real estate equity for an immediate discount? That same $50,000 you were going to stick in an ETF or whatever can land you real property with $100,000 or more of equity available between the immediate sales price and the debt owed. No speculation, lucky rabbit's foot nor sleepless nights required.

3) Real estate is risky because too many factors are beyond your control.

This one holds a kernel of truth, but it misses how easy it is to manage the risk. We're not shooting from the hip when we purchase real estate. We're data-mining thousands of off-market property records every month and then plucking the diamonds from the rough.

And we're doing so before the competition comes calling and starts a bidding war. With this approach, you can stack the deck in your favor before you ever sign on the dotted line.

When you have a 1,000+ potential leads in a city but only enough capital to invest in one or two properties, you can be quite selective. You only touch the cream of the crop: those investments with the most available equity, the fewest risk factors and located in the highest demand neighborhoods. In short, the safe bets that will pay off even if the market suddenly tanks. Really, this business only gets risky when you're managing so much capital that you have to target lower equity homes just to put all your money to work. But isn't that a good problem to have?

4) The market is too crowded. Too many investors and not enough inventory to make a steady profit nowadays.

The "market" has nothing more to do with equity hunting than the price of venison at the grocery store affects the hunter's aim. What does it matter to you how many investors are cruising Zillow and the MLS looking for deals? They aren't your competitors. You're stalking a completely different hunting ground.

We're pulling our investments out of the wilderness and bringing them *to* the marketplace for the first time. Whether renting or flipping, sustainable success comes from smart bidding at foreclosure, HOA and tax auctions, or finding and finessing distressed homeowners that aren't yet selling their homes to transfer title and let you do that for them.

As for inventory, if there isn't enough on-market housing to meet local demand, then that's even better for you. Less competition and you can command higher prices for the "meat" you brought to market.

If there's a local seller's market, with way too many homes up for sale, then an equity *jaeger* is also sitting pretty. With all the data about recent and pending sales available, it'll be even easier for you to estimate a fast selling price and only hunt the "big game" properties that will return plenty of equity when you take them into this crowded market.

5) I don't have serious money nor connections. There's no way to compete with the big players and real estate sure isn't a game for amateurs.

I have to admit I fell for this myth myself when first starting out. Oh, I was so intimidated. Probably would have thrown in the towel before closing on the first deal if my partner hadn't steadied my nerves. I felt like some primitive little primate scurrying between the stomping legs of dinosaurs, doing my best to hustle a few scraps while not getting flattened.

At least at first. It didn't take long to see why the mighty reptiles are extinct and we evolved into the ultimate apex predator.

When I actually started duking it out with the big money players at auctions, negotiating deals directly with banks and mortgage servicers or fighting foreclosure lawyers in court, I realized these lumbering dinosaurs didn't stand a chance against me.

Not because I'm some sort of real estate ninja, but simply because I have two insurmountable advantages in my corner that the "big boys" could never match. And you'll have these powers as well, regardless of your starting skill level.

1) The Power of Focus. All the big players, from investment fund asset managers to the bank reps themselves, are working hundreds, if not thousands of deals at a time. There's simply no way they can give each investment the hands-on research, evaluation and shepherding it requires. There aren't enough hours in the day. So either they're delegating crucial details to less experienced assistants or they're skipping the minutia all together.

Contrast that with a nimble entrepreneur like you, who will only be working one, or at most a handful of deals at a time. Unlike the overworked big companies, you have time to manually check the comps and not rely exclusively on 3rd party software. You can drive out to your prospective properties and see them with your own eyes. Walk around with your home inspector and contractors and let them show you what they're talking about instead of just skimming a report in your office.

You won't be sending out mass direct mail flyers, instead you'll be engaged in long, detailed conversations with distressed homeowners, learning deep insights into the property, finding their pain points and building rapport. My goodness, you even have the luxury of actually reading the contracts you're signing! To say nothing of sitting down with your lawyer face to face and going through your options point by point.

Time to take your time is something that money can't buy and experience can't replace.

2) The Power of Motivation. Not only will you have the luxury of taking your time to study carefully everything you're doing and seek advice for things you don't understand yet, you'll be far more motivated to do so in more detail and more often than any big competitor. If you think that's a quaint notion, take a look at the lenders you're negotiating with or the other cash investors you're racing against. Never mind the company's reputation. Think about the individuals managing particular deals.

Despite their experience, these people are just employees of a large corporate machine. There's no personal motivator to their work and investments, other than general professional pride and a broad drive to advance their career. It's not like their money and reputation are on the line when they sign a deal, so where's the pressure to go the extra mile? The only pressure they have comes from their management and partners, constantly pushing them to hurry up with current tasks and move on to the next Big Priority. Even if they're earning commissions, they'll still be ever conscious of the time they're putting into a particular project. The urge to wrap things up fast and move on to something else, no matter how much they earn, is always at the back of their mind and sapping their motivation.

Compare that mindset to your hunger. You're not a corporate equity hunter working by the hour or for a cut of the harvest. You're hunting equity to eat. For professional survival. That means you'll dive into every detail of a deal and do whatever it takes to minimize risk and maximize profit.

And since risk management and return on investment in this business all comes down to who is willing to put in the most time to gather more data on a property, you'll have a vast advantage in every deal. A hungry amateur with the time to crunch the numbers and the passion to learn will always outperform the busy, distracted professional who just needs to hit some minimum performance metrics every quarter to keep the boss off their back.

6) You need to be good at fixing up dilapidated properties to make any serious money in real estate.

While a lot of people use the terms interchangeably, "bringing properties to market" and "fix and flip" are two separate niches, each with their own unique strategies. We're focusing on the safer rehab of buying off-market properties and unlocking their equity by bringing them on-market. Here, we find homes that are in a livable, if not quite sellable state already, where the main problem is that they're occupied by "distressed" owners that don't have the means nor interest to sell the place or rent it out.

Our goal is simply to get the properties up to selling or renting standards as fast and cheaply as possible. Yes, some strategic and precise "rehab" work is always required. Minor stuff such as fixing wear and tear issues, worn carpet and outdated appliances, and then enhancing curb appeal through quick landscaping and paint jobs. But we're not trying to create new value through significant renovations, only maximizing the home's current value in the most cost-effective way possible. While there are some exceptions, as a general rule of thumb, if you're investing more money into rehabilitating a property than you spent acquiring it, then you did something wrong.

This whole process is not as "fun" or "sexy" as buying dirt-cheap damaged properties and nursing them back to life. Instead of tiling a bathroom or knocking down walls, you're creating value by poring over Excel spreadsheets for hidden equity and negotiating with creditors for a cheaper payoff. No one is going to make a reality TV show about a flipper who spends 99% of their work day on the phone or glued to a computer screen. So I hope you aren't looking for fame in this business, but you can at least take solace in the fortune.

When you're purchasing existing equity at a discount and bringing the property to a sellable state, instead of trying to create equity through new construction and renovation, then you're taking on far less risk. Maybe your per-deal rate of return is smaller, but your overall business will flourish. You can make smaller but safer deals far more often and compound your returns in no time at all. No offense to the amazing fix 'em and flip 'em entrepreneurs out there that make it work. I admire what they do, but that niche isn't for me. I'm not that sort of risk-taker.

I don't know about you, but I'll stick to just rehabbing ok properties into good sellers, since we can do that faster, cheaper and more frequently than someone who's fixing up disaster properties into great sellers.

PHASE ONE:
Laying The Foundation For
Lasting Success

Why Do So Many Real Estate Professionals Fail?

"Shallow men believe in luck. Strong men believe in cause and effect."

- Ralph Waldo Emerson

Like any business endeavor, there are countless little mistakes new and even seasoned players can make that will cost them money. Still, complete failure in this industry can usually be traced back to an investor buying into one of the great real estate fallacies. Even if you're not yet involved and have only done some casual googling of house flipping and residential rental strategies, I'm sure you've seen these dangerous myths perpetuated by all the so-called real estate "gurus" out there:

House flipping or property rentals are a <u>low risk</u> source of <u>passive income</u> that <u>only takes</u> good ol' fashioned American pluck, grit and determination to make millions.

Boy, oh, boy. I could write a hundred books about all the fortunes lost by new investors that fell prey to that naïve fantasy. Nearly fell for the hype myself a time or two when I was first starting out. Now, of course real estate investment can be a lucrative field, even better than the stock market. After all, what decent stock trades at a price half or less than the company's equity? Yet such deals are easy to find in distressed, off-market real estate.

I'm proof of how a regular Joe can make a consistent and excellent living from this niche, so I'm sure not trying to scare you off... but just like with any entrepreneurial endeavor, having the right mindset and being free of self-deception are just as important success factors as raising capital or refining your business strategy.

I've seen too many ultra-motivated new investors believe the hype from all the reality TV shows and endless "X tips to make millions flipping houses" articles on the internet, or listen to all those radio shows where some "genius" is laying out their "system"... which usually involves a membership fee of some sort. These normally level-headed investors then dive straight into this business with their minds full of dreams and vague generic advice, only to crash and burn when the real-world headwinds strike, usually torching their retirement and life savings in the process. And all that carnage could have been avoided if they went into this business clear-eyed and without any BS fantasies clouding their judgment.

If you're reading this book, then you've already taken a giant leap to ensure that no matter what happens, you won't wind up broken and ruined like thousands of other wannabe investors. At the end of the day, the real difference between happy, successful professionals and bitter, bankrupt amateurs has nothing to do with innate skill or luck; it's all about whether or not they sought out and applied the hard-earned advice of the bloodied investors that went before them.

As an investment advisor, it's my mission to mentor my clients above all else. I'm not here to hype up or motivate them, but rather arm my clients with the knowledge and mindset of a savvy investor. To turn amateurs into shrewd professionals who know how to take the guesswork out of making an investment and manage all forms of risk, all while finding value and creating new equity in the process.

Real estate investing is not some "gentleman's game." Especially nowadays with so many cash-rich flippers fighting over an ever-shrinking pool of distressed properties. This world is a jungle on the best of days, and an outright battlefield most of the time. While the mental preparation will take far more work than just reading a few pages in a book, let me at least dispel these common myths that turn so many otherwise smart investors into lambs being led to slaughter. We'll cover step-by-step how to avoid these landmines and more in Part 2, but the first step is to rid your mind of all the hype around flipping homes for a living:

1) Real estate is the exact opposite of "passive income."

Whether you focus on quick flips or long-term renting, you will work your butt off for every dollar you earn. This may be an old industry, but your business is a startup. And have you ever heard a successful entrepreneur brag about how little they work?

When renting, your involvement never ends. Even with a reliable property management company to handle the mundane details, you're still ultimately the landlord, with all the liabilities that entails. So delegate oversight at your own risk. When flipping, no matter how great a team you assembled, you still must know what to pay for an investment, find ways to create value by resolving legal and physical issues cheaply, all while coordinating renovations, agents, lawyers, etc.

At best, if you are not intimately involved in every stage of the operation, then you're exposing yourself to all sorts of new risks. At worst, you're setting yourself up to get ripped off. Remember, before you can collect a payday, there are so many hands reaching into your pockets, such as lawyers, taxmen, contractors, etc. So if you aren't carefully fact-checking, documenting and managing everything that's going on, you'll find yourself pulling out nothing but lint from your pockets when the day's over.

If you're employing a pro investment advisor, also make sure to hire them *before* you even make a bid on your first house. To get your money's worth out of their service, you want their advice on how to avoid making mistakes in the first place, not how to clean up the mess.

It might seem like a small note, but agents and advisors should be employed as preventive medicine and not as troubleshooters after you've ran into a problem. Afterall, the old "an ounce of prevention is worth a pound of cure" saw takes on a whole new level of meaning when you have hundreds of thousands of your own dollars on the line.

Naturally, a great agent can relieve much of this micro-management pressure, but you still can't delegate everything. Plus, the truly reliable professional agents with a long list of references don't come cheap.

2) Real estate is the very definition of a high-risk investment.

With the margins so tight and so many potential issues that could pop up, many of which are out of your control, there is precious little room for error in this business. Again, I'll cover the detailed do's and don'ts in Part 2, but it's crucial for investors to fully grasp the risks involved at a visceral level, and to understand why ruthless risk management is what separates the pros from the bankrupt.

The greatest risks come from:

- Overestimating the amount of equity in a position.

- Overestimating the property's value.

- Failing to realistically estimate your total costs over time.

- Over renovating properties.

While often overlooked by real estate investing guides, the hands-down biggest risk is not knowing how much equity is in a property before you even purchase. If you know that and only stick to properties with generous cushions of equity, then even if you make a mistake somewhere else, you'll still come out of every deal with a profit. That right there is the secret to my success.

Maybe the home's value will appreciate later, maybe not. Doesn't matter either way because we aren't in the business of speculating on prices. If that's what excites you, then you should put your money into the stock market. As a professional real estate investor though, your business is to hunt down hidden equity before a property gets to market, and create new value through smart renovations and clearing debt cheaply. We don't place bets on the future and hope for the best. We buy properties that can generate instant profit now and bet that we can create more profit later, but even if we're wrong there's a generous cushion of existing wealth to limit our risk.

I'll go into the specifics of tracking down off-market discounts later, but professional flippers will never place a bid unless there's already a comfortable equity spread at the current market value. Even then they want to see extra opportunities to add even more value before prioritizing this project above any others. So if you're wrong about any aspect of the equity evaluation process, then you're dead in the water from the get-go. Anything else you do later can only limit your losses, but likely won't ever return a profit.

With that said, knowing the current equity and potential equity you can add isn't a matter of guesswork. It's a straightforward list of due diligence items to check, with only a small potential margin of error. You've probably heard all the caveats from different "gurus" saying you'll never be completely sure what a property is worth... but that just shows how little they truly understand the details of flipping residential properties. In the last nine years, I've sold 95% of my 300+ flips at exactly the price I originally estimated I could move them for. This has nothing to do with luck, nor do I have some magic "system" or secret formula.

It's all a numbers game, and I just do my homework. Granted, my niche is structuring deals in unique ways to unlock maximum value from the property's debt load, but that wouldn't even be possible without careful analysis to find out how much value is hidden in the current price. You can replicate this same success by following the straightforward principals I lay out in this guide, and then scale things up by seeking out the right mentorship.

This is why a great investment advisor—by great I mean one that has been in the trenches and flipped houses themselves and didn't just read about the process—will rein in your enthusiasm in the planning stages and ensure you leave plenty of wiggle room in every phase of the process. Especially making sure you limit your financial leverage, include a realistic margin of error in your valuation, sell pricing and renovation estimates, and above all, creating a flexible exit strategy to guarantee you can pull out with a profit even if everything turns against you. In short, realistic risk management.

3) Real estate requires far more than just cash on hand and a "go getter" attitude.

Let's face the cold hard reality: you aren't going to discover great investment candidates by cruising the Multiple Listing Service (MLS) or the For Sale By Owner listings on Zillow. The market is just too efficient for any lucrative "arbitrage" opportunities to stay available to the general public for long. So if you find a great deal that seems too good to be true, odds are it is and you're missing some nasty surprise. Usually in the form of some hard to find lien on the property or structural/site issue that a typical home inspection wouldn't discover.

Even if there is a large mismatch between the asking price and market value, without any hidden problems, the big players, including Zillow itself in some hot markets, will scoop these deals up faster than you can. Even if you're quick, you'll find yourself in a nasty bidding war against competitors with ample cash reserves. Sure, maybe you can get lucky, happens occasionally, but hoping to get lucky is not an investing strategy—that's what gamblers do. So if you're dreaming of simply searching the internet for cheap houses in expensive neighborhoods and expect to hit the jackpot, then you're better off staying out of the real estate game all together. Just take your cash and head off to a casino. You'll have more fun that way... and probably lose less money.

However, if you're serious about building a real estate empire and want to minimize risk while maximizing reward, then you need focus. Especially if you follow all the data mining steps I'll outline shortly, you'll be overwhelmed by all the opportunities and will spread yourself too thin in a hurry. Just like with any business, you must focus your efforts on some niche to build a competitive advantage. Now this niche is much easier to create than it sounds. It doesn't mean being the best at everything, but just finding one thing you can either do better than average or at least what you're most interested in, and then pour your energy into dominating that field.

The first thing a pro investment advisor will have you do is figure out your "niche," or edge. There are countless niches you could carve out, but they all revolve around maintaining some type of data advantage. In other words, having some unique information or insight into a slice of the market that isn't common knowledge. We'll go over in detail how to find and hone your advantage in Part 2, but the key right now is to realize how incredibly competitive this industry is. If you don't have an edge, you don't have a business plan. And if you're planning on luck, you're planning to fail.

Equity Is Investing 101 Stuff, So Why Won't I Shut Up About It?

I realize we've just started and I've probably used the term equity a hundred times already. I'm aiming for a thousand before we're done.

Equity is far more than just a simple statistic, the difference between an investment's market value and the price you bought it for. Equity is the be-all and end-all of our decision making and risk management process. Again, you might understand that intellectually, but it's crucial you grasp this concept on an instinctual gut level to guarantee your success in any sort of market conditions.

Equity Versus Profit – Why You Need A New Bottom Line.

The typical real estate investor places profit first and foremost in all investment decisions. Maybe they're calculating the rate of return on investment (ROI) or the cash on cash return or something else, but it all comes back to the bottom line question of, "How much can I earn on this deal versus another?" Risk is assessed separately and often subjectively, with the goal of finding some optimum balance between risk and reward.

And this logic seems to make sense. Afterall, profit is the ultimate goal, so if we ever take our eyes off the prize, aren't we just setting ourselves up for failure? The only way to maximize profit is to maximize the rate of return on every dollar we spend, right?

That mindset is fine for a CEO choosing where to allocate operating capital in the future, but it's misleading for an investor who's trying to decide which discounted property is the "best" deal to pour money into. Focusing on profit ignores the subtlety of what you're buying when investing in real estate.

We're purchasing equity interest in a position. We're buying an abstract legal concept, with the goal of selling that stake on the open market and turning it into real cash. Maybe this means we'll actually take title to the property; sometimes we only need a partial interest (more on this in Phase 2).

In either case, the amount of equity we'll have left over after the expenses of entering and exiting the position is all that matters. Some level of profit will always flow from a high-equity position no matter what happens because:

- The more equity you have, the faster you can sell and speed inventory turnover. Would you rather earn 100% profit on one deal a year, or 10-20% on each of 10 deals? Compound returns works just like compound interest here.

- If you're renting, more equity gives you more leverage to negotiate lower debt payoffs, thereby increasing your income, or at least more capital you can raise from a line of credit on your assets to finance new deals.

- More equity gives you a financial cushion in case of trouble. Let the market do whatever it does, because you have the wiggle room to still turn a profit.

So in practice, if we do a great job researching the property and bringing it to market, then we'll create even more profit than what we estimated in equity, due to fast inventory turnover or lower holding costs when renting.

If we do only a good job, then equity and profit will be synonymous. At most differing by a few percentage points.

However, if we make a mistake or the market throws some random curveball, then the more equity we have, the safer we are. Just like an airbag. You don't ever plan on needing it, but would you buy a car that didn't have one? And just as important for risk analysis, we can use equity to quantify the risk differential between two alternative deals instead of just guessing.

For example, say we only have the funds for one deal, but have two good leads to choose from. Assume both properties are identical and located on the same block.

Option A: $80,000 investment, including taking ownership, rehab, holding and closing costs. Estimated equity after reselling with a clear title: $70,000.

Option B: $40,000 investment, including taking ownership, rehab, holding and closing costs. Estimated equity after reselling with a clear title: $40,000.

A profit-oriented analysis would choose option B because of its 100% return over option A versus the 88% return there. The supplemental risk analysis would even conclude that option B is a safer move, since only half the capital is at risk.

An equity-based approach would choose option A for several key reasons completely ignored by the profit analysis:

1) The larger store of equity lowers risk, since if we need to, we can absorb unexpected expenses or accept a lowering selling price and still turn a comfortable profit. The safety margin with Option B is only 57% as large, so a much riskier investment even though it ties up less capital.

2) When striking a deal with the mortgage lender or other debt holders, the first option gives you more negotiating room and better returns. For example, for each deal you worked out a short payoff settlement with the original mortgage owner that cuts 10% from the amount owed. You generate an extra $7k in equity from the first deal, but only $4k from the second.

3) Inventory turnover speed. Since you have so much equity, you can accept a fast, but lower priced offer. This lets you reduce holding costs and complete more deals throughout the year, hence compounding returns. For example, say you accept a low offer that knocked 20% from your equity, but allowed you to close in just 2-3 months instead of the six months you planned. So you lose $14k in potential profit, or likely $10k because of your lower holding costs and closing costs... but now you have time and free cash to do both option A and option B deals instead of just one, compounding your returns far more than the $10k you "left on the table."

Equity Is How We Keep From Speculating

The demand for properties in a particular location or the likelihood that local home values are going to rise are really secondary factors. Yes, we'll trade information with local agents, but that's just to more accurately update our estimated equity. For example, refining our price target and better estimate our holding costs by seeing how long it will take to move the property. The safest way to "speculate" on the future is to buy only properties that you could sell immediately at a profit, with only a bare minimum of staging costs. And not just a bit in the black, but deep enough to cushion you from surprises.

Unlike all these speculative guesses about what's going to happen or not happen to your local market in the future, we can quantify equity using current data with a high degree of accuracy. Maybe all your dreams will come true and the property will skyrocket in value like you hope, but that's not a safe and sustainable way to make investment decisions. At best, this is an extremely advanced niche that requires some form of insider knowledge. At worst, it's little more than gambling.

The specific methods we'll use might get complicated, but the overall investment decision process is simple. Notice that every single step of real estate investing all centers on equity.

1) Scrape the online market value and debt load of as many off-market properties (from auctions and pre-foreclosures) that we can, then calculate the equity available in each position.

2) Filter the dataset by removing a variety of risk factors that could affect the equity estimate.

3) Make offers to only those properties with the most equity.

4) Refine your equity estimate with on-site inspections and other due diligence before closing.

5) Grow the equity by bringing the property to market or get renters in as fast and cheaply as possible while negotiating for lower settlements from debt holders.

6) Rinse and repeat as many times as you can throughout the year, rolling as much of your profit as you can afford back into the business

to save on taxes and compound returns... thus generating more equity in your own company.

Equity is Risk Management Quantified

I know I've talked a big game about "never being surprised," but let's face it, eventually you will be surprised. No one's perfect. We all make mistakes, and that's before the world throws random curve balls at you. You can stack the deck in your favor so that the odds of turning a profit on any deal are 99%... but that 1% will catch up with you sometime. Usually at the worst possible time.

The only way to come close to guaranteeing success even in the most extreme of worst-case scenarios is to only work with deals that have plenty of excess equity to begin with.

Some examples:

I invested $80k in my initial purchase price, plus rehab and staging in a pre-foreclosure in a bland cookie cutter subdivision. If I'll have $50k in equity left over after closing and lender payoff costs, I'm not going to quibble if I get an offer that's $20k less than my asking price the same month I first listed the property.

I'll likely take the $30k profit, knowing I can now flip two high-equity investments in the time frame I planned for just one and increase my profits far more than the $20k I might be leaving on the table. Or I can hold out a bit longer for a better price, knowing I can still exit the deal fast with a decent ROI at any time.

However, let's say I chose to invest a bit less into a poor-equity deal because I had a gut feeling for whatever reason that home prices were going to jump in a certain neighborhood. In one month, not much has changed in the market, but I received the same offer at $20k less than asking. After adding up my remaining equity, I see I'll only break even or earn just a paltry return. So I ignore the offer and hold out for more.

Now I am no longer an investor. I'm a speculator.

That's not some minor semantic difference but rather a whole new ball game. I'm accepting a huge new level of risk, so I need a bigger reward to justify it, which means I need to take more risks to see that payoff and so on in a teetering circle. Maybe everything works out like

I planned and I make a killing. Doubling or tripling what I could have made in the first scenario. Maybe one of the million things that are out of my control keeps my plan from coming to fruition in a reasonable time frame, so I wind up selling at a loss just to limit the damage as my holding costs pile up.

Either way, no respectable risk management plan has so many "maybe's" in it. The only way to protect yourself is to stick to the "unsexy" but higher-equity investments, even if those returns are measured in the humble 20-30% range instead of the lofty 200-300% cloud level.

Equity Opens Up Endless Opportunities, Even In Supposedly Over-Crowded Markets.

One of the many beautiful things about focusing on equity above all else is that profit-making opportunities are always there for the taking. You don't have to read the tea leaves and figure out if the local housing market is going to go boom or bust soon, let alone care about interest rates rising or falling. I get all the headline news I need from the numbers my web crawlers are scraping from the clerk of court's and property appraiser's websites every night.

If the local economy is healthy and you're in a seller's market, then rising home values will automatically give you more equity in an investment, even if your acquisition costs are going up. If you're in a housing crash, with home values plummeting fast, then that's an even better buying market with so many distressed sellers ready to transfer title for next to nothing. Not to mention lenders willing to negotiate payoffs for pennies on the dollar. With so little invested on your part, you can negotiate a great short sale/short payoff with the bank or flip fast to wholesale or retail homebuyers. Or just find a renter while riding out the crisis.

And in the rare chance that the market stays neutral, neither a buyer's nor seller's market? Then you have peace of mind that your equity and home value estimates will be even more exact. Let the market go up, down or sideways—equity-obsessed investors will always come out on top.

As of this writing (2018), the American housing market is booming. Foreclosures are near record lows, with only about 1 in every 2,500 housing units in the US entering the foreclosure process every month.[2] At the same time, it seems like everyone and their mother is hanging out a "We buy houses as-is, fast and in cash" sign. At first glance, it hardly seems like the right time to dive into the market, but it's never been a better time if you follow the pre-foreclosure, equity-hunting game plan I lay out here.

Even in these supposedly "bleak" times, opportunity abounds for those taking their research a step further and not waiting for official foreclosure judgments to come in before starting a direct mailing campaign. Despite the healthy economy, 3% of all single-family residential mortgages are in default longer than 30 days.[3] Might not sound like much, but here are millions of the most popular and easiest to sell properties in pre-foreclosure right now. Long before most investors and agents have even heard of them. I can't even begin to calculate how many tens of billions of dollars' worth of equity is just sitting around for the taking. We're talking Warren Buffett levels of wealth waiting on you to save it before all that equity is wiped out by attorney fees, interest and auction sales.

The More Equity You Have, The Easier It Is To Unlock Even More.

We touched on this before, but it's worth repeating. There are so many ways to squeeze out extra equity through simple legal maneuvering as well, especially if you want to hold onto the property long-term as a rental investment. Now, this is its own niche, so we really don't have the space here, but I cover the most lucrative tricks in my online workshop course.

---

[2] RealtyTrac. (November 2018). U.S. Real Estate Trends & Market Info https://www.realtytrac.com/statsandtrends/foreclosuretrends/

[3] Board of Governors of the Federal Reserve System (U.S.), Delinquency Rate on Single-Family Residential Mortgages, Booked in Domestic Offices, All Commercial Banks [DRSFRMACBS], retrieved from FRED, Federal Reserve Bank of St. Louis; https://fred.stlouisfed.org/series/DRSFRMACBS Dec. 12, 2018.

The key point to remember is that before things reach the Lis Pendens level, you can bet the original mortgage promissory note has been resold many times and passed through several different mortgage servicers. Each time this happens, there's a high chance of some clerical error that can undermine the mortgage lender's interest in court. Or even cause outright violations of various consumer protection laws. I don't want to name names, but if you follow the news, then you can see how this is extra true with certain high-profile lenders that have a, shall we say, checkered history with protecting their customers.

And that's just the tip of the iceberg, since banks and credit unions only issue 49% of all residential mortgages. The other 51% of mortgages originate with non-bank lenders.[4] Online firms, other investors, seller financing, etc... These lenders tend to be far more flexible and amenable to a variety of settlement offers.

Even if you're dealing with an uncaring bureaucratic monolith that won't even return your calls, you're never completely out of options to get them to the bargaining table. For a simplified example, every time the mortgage is sold on the secondary market, the homeowner must be notified in writing within a certain time frame. Can the current mortgage servicer provide documentation proving that every debt owner in the chain properly notified the homeowner in time? Because if not, there's a $2,000 fine for each violation of the homeowner's legal rights. Since the original mortgage has changed hands 10 times, perhaps a countersuit for $20,000 could get to the bottom of things... unless the current mortgage holder is willing to settle by forgiving $5,000 from the amount owed.

And there you just plucked extra equity out of thin air. For a savvy attorney, there are hundreds of other examples. Despite all their money, these multi-billion-dollar corporations have only a handful of lawyers processing thousands of defaults at a time, while you're focused on just one case at a time. Gives you quite an edge over the "big dogs." This type of legal maneuvering is kind of my passion, and

---

[4] Mortgage Daily. 2018. "Mortgage Daily 2017 Biggest Lender Ranking" [Press Release] Retrieved from https://globenewswire.com/news-release/2018/03/26/1453033/0/en/Mortgage-Daily-2017-Biggest-Lender-Ranking.html.

huge source of income, but you should also consult with an attorney that specializes in foreclosure litigation to see all the options available to you.

But I Don't Have Any Capital And Can Barely Pay My Own Rent. How Can I Build Up A War Chest To Play With The Big Boys?

We don't have the space here for an in-depth exploration of all the myriad ways you can raise capital for this enterprise. Really, private equity and venture capital financing is its own ultra-specialized niche, but here's an overview of straightforward ways anyone can raise funds for your new startup besides just saving up your cash.

Partnerships

This classic equity-financing arrangement is incredibly flexible. Whenever possible, try to partner with someone that brings both capital and core competency skills to the business, like I had the good fortune to do. However, that's not strictly required. Quite often, real estate ventures consist of a network of "silent" partners providing initial capital, with just a single managing partner handling all the investments. You can even set up an S corporation for casual investors that want a share of the profits, but want to limit their liability.

No matter how you arrange the business though, the key is to not make decisions by committee. Always keep your partners in the loop, of course. Seek their advice and actually listen to it, but at the end of the day a single person must be responsible for "pulling the trigger" on when to enter or exit a position and at what price point. If one person doesn't have authority to adapt to rapidly changing circumstances or negotiate with homeowners on the spot, then you're giving up your flexibility and will be at a disadvantage compared to more nimble individual cash investors.

Foreign investment

This isn't as complicated as you might think. You don't have to seek out the investors yourself. In this scenario, you're usually working with a 3rd party wealth management firm, family office or regional developmental center. They will bring in the foreign money; your task is just to prove you can put it to good use.

This is an especially lucrative source of funding if you're operating in a rural or low-income urban area. The US government's EB-5 Immigrant Investor Program offers green cards for rich foreigners, excuse me, "High Net Worth Individuals," that are willing to invest at least $500,000 in one of the 900 regional development centers across the US. The program is in high demand, usually with more money chasing projects than there are opportunities available at any given moment.

It's worth checking out the USCIS.gov site for an up-to-date list of regional centers you can contact and pitch your services to.

Financing

If you absolutely need to raise funds through debt-financing, then do so before your purchase your first investment. Leverage your personal assets, such as a second home loan, 401k loan, maxing out lines of credit, etc… to build up your seed money. In my early days in this business I even maxed out my credit cards. I would definitely not recommend that, but it's still better and safer than taking out a mortgage to invest in on-market properties.

As you build your business, you can leverage your long-term rental properties for new financing to scale fast, but never take out a mortgage to purchase a property. Even if you can find a lender willing to finance a short-term flip at a reasonable rate, you're throwing away all the flexibility and speed advantages that go along with cash.

Scaled growth

The riskiest point in real estate is when an investor has been so successful that they have too much capital to invest. If you only have $100,000 available, it's fairly easy to sort through all the opportunities in your community and chase after the top two or three best deals. When you have $10 million or more in assets under management, you'll swamp the local market and have to scrape the bottom of the equity bucket to find a job for your cash. So naturally, these big firms have to branch out well beyond their comfort zone to put that money to good use. Well, you investors up in New York or San Francisco chuckled just then, since you probably spend more than that just on flipping parking places, but for most real estate companies, this is a problem. They need local partners.

Which opens up a sweet opportunity for us equity hunters to swoop in and add value for everyone. As you're poring over your web-scraped data, you'll notice a ton of out-of-state private equity firms getting burned on local deals. You have nothing to lose by contacting them and introducing yourself. Run the numbers on their poor investments as if they were one of yours and share the results.

Show them where they miscalculated equity or any other way they could have profited. You can start small, acting as a commission-based local investment adviser. After a few successful deals though, don't accept their offer to work for them full-time. Instead, offer them a ground-floor investment in your latest fund. The opportunities are endless.

How To Build A Market-Dominating Team & Business On A Budget.

No matter what you've seen on TV, no successful house-flipping operation is a mom and pop operation. At least not for long. It may begin like that, but lasting success comes from building up your own infrastructure so you don't have to rely on 3rd parties and can scale up your business.

Successful flipping takes more than just skill at finding discounted homes and identifying value. It's an intricate, complicated business that requires a whole legal, construction, financial and advisement support network to work. Most especially when you want to scale up and make real money by flipping multiple properties at once. You need a well-oiled system in place to not only lower your operating costs but keep all these moving parts from running out of control.

For example, in my team, we have a network of investors to provide all the cash necessary so we don't have to handcuff ourselves to financial lenders. We have in-house lawyers to tackle all the myriad legal and title issues, a dedicated research team to handle the grunt work of data mining and our own realtors to stage and sell the properties. Last, but most definitely not least, we partner with an exclusive licensed contractor in each market. That ensures we're always working with the same professionals on each house, and the contractor's long-term financial success is tied to our own. A win-win for everyone.

This all gives us maximum control and flexibility on every deal, while keeping costs down well below what most retail real estate investors struggle with.

But it wasn't always like that. I understand how daunting it feels to build such an operation from scratch… because I've been there. But unlike Max and I, if you apply the lessons in this book, you can skip most of the growing pains and start on third base.

Whether you're a real estate startup or looking to scale up, the team you're working with will make or break you. That's why the most effective and long-lasting investment outfits are partnerships, where each partner brings a unique skill set that covers part of the investing practice so that as little as possible is outsourced to freelancers.

Even if you're unable to find reliable partners, there are several steps you can take to build a team that will give even the smallest player an edge over the biggest investment firms in the business.

Knowledge

The very first item to invest in is yourself. Partners, lawyers, analysis software, web crawlers and virtual assistants are all crucial to saving time, avoiding mistakes and scaling up your business, but they're no substitute for mastering all the details yourself.

This book is obviously a great start, but no single guide can cover everything. Whether you take your education to the next level by diving into my online workshop and videos or not, you need to invest serious time and money seeking professional advice. I'm not saying don't risk any money until you're an expert on every aspect of this business, since obviously that's not going to happen until you pull the trigger and dive into the market. I'm saying make sure you keep studying every single day, building up an invaluable store of knowledge that will eventually spill over into real world profit.

Wealth and health come and go, but insider knowledge is a perpetual power and success generating machine. In any industry, a man or woman who knows something that others don't can create value from nothing just by putting their information out there. Even if they're financially broke and physically weak, they'll still dominate their field in short order.

With that said, building confidence in yourself and knowledge base is just as important. As you go through this book, "paper trade" using the steps provided on real properties to practice your new skills. That's a crucial step we take in the workshop videos and you can reproduce for free at home.

For example, don't just take my word on how to set a realistic selling price or estimate. Pick a random property in your home country that's going up for auction and fill in the spreadsheets and checklists. Work the numbers yourself and watch the property. See what price the new owners list at and where it actually sold. Call up the agent or investor and see if they're willing to answer some questions. You'll be surprised what you can learn and the confidence you'll find in your own skills over a friendly chat. Everyone likes to brag, and let's be honest, the humble don't usually get into real estate investing!

Data Services and Assistants

No matter what niche you focus on, data is your secret weapon. The more you know about a property, it's legal history and the parties currently holding interest, the better you can estimate equity, manage risk and create new value without investing more money. There is no such thing as trivia in this business. Maybe not everything is equally important, but you'll be amazed at the big picture you can piece together by all these tidbits before anyone else does.

The obvious downside is this process soon becomes too much for anyone to handle by themselves. Thankfully, we're in the 21st century and it's never been easier for a "mom and pop" operation to build a sophisticated, efficient and scalable administrative "back end." And do so without breaking the budget.

I'll show you later where in each step all these services come into play, how to use them and some recommended providers. Right now you need to understand that the following items aren't luxuries, but basic tools of the trade. A modern real estate investor that doesn't invest at least a few hundred dollars into these bare minimum resources is as ready for success as a carpenter showing up to work without a hammer.

- A reliable prime administrative assistant for sensitive information. Ideally, this is an in-house employee, but you can find reliable online freelancers in the beginning if need be.

- A team of online virtual assistants for data mining and customer care.

- Subscriptions to web-scraping firms or hire a freelance programmer to design and run your own.

- Skip tracing subscription for lead generation.

Webscraping

Even in a healthy economy, a middle-sized metropolitan area will have hundreds, if not thousands of Lis Pendens and Notices of Defaults filed into the public records every month. There's just no way you can manually research, screen and filter all this data for equity opportunities and leads by yourself. Thankfully, it's never been easier or cheaper to hire a 3rd party automation service that will "scrape" each county's website for the information you need and send you it to you in the format you like. Then keep doing so every single day.

I can't stress how important this step is to success in this business. No matter your other skills, the "formula" for guaranteeing profits in any market comes down to finding deals and generating leads before everyone else. Webscraping is the fastest and most affordable option to find diamonds in the ruff. This might seem to be a dubious or excessively complicated step when you're just starting out, but let me clear up some of the common myths:

- Webscraping is 100% legal in this context. We are merely automating the search of already public records and not violating any privacy laws nor any commercial website's terms of service.

- No coding experienced is required. There are many off-the-shelf solutions you can purchase from business intelligence firms, or even hire a freelance programmer to design your own custom scripts.

- It's not complicated to make use of this data. All you do is press the "sync" or "run" command and wait for your data to be pulled and dropped into an Excel spreadsheet.

- The costs are miniscule. Compared to all the hours of manual labor you're saving, you'll make back your initial investment within a month or two.

Hiring Freelancers Best Practices

If you've employed freelancers in the past from sites like Upwork.com, Freelancer.com or Guru.com then you probably understand the incredible value these folks offer. Taking advantage of this vast talent pool of specialty hired guns that you can snatch up in minutes for the most random of jobs will take your business to a whole new level. It's what the military calls a "force multiplier."

If you're new to hiring and managing freelancers, then take some time to create a free account at these marketplaces and peruse the talent. Virtual assistants, programmers, graphic artists, researchers... the opportunities are endless. And the rules for screening and hiring quality workers are much simpler than finding quality employees. The exact details of what you're looking for obviously vary depending upon the type of task, but if you follow these general rules of thumb you can't go wrong:

- Make your job description as detailed as possible. Explicitly list every task you want done, the standard of quality you expect and most of all, what you envision the end result to look like. Besides saving a ton of time going back and forth in interviews and making sure you get accurate quotes to compare, these people have worked with many different clients with problems similar to your own. You'll be surprised how often these specialists notice something important in your workflow that you overlooked. Or even a better way to do things all together.

- Stick to freelancers who have earned at least five-figures on the website you're posting a job in. Yes, many freelancers have a day-job and are doing this on the side. Others are full-time independent workers who find their clients through multiple websites. Others are brand new to freelancing. It's sometimes hard to tell, so to be on the safe side, stick to people that have been around on a particular website long enough to earn a few grand. The more they've earned on a platform, the less likely they are to jeopardize their reputation there.

- When evaluating their work history, reviews from past clients are more important than portfolio items. Assuming you actually read the reviews on the freelancer's profile and not only the star rating. What's 5-star work for one person might be subpar for your standards. Usually the biggest concern isn't performance, but rather time management issues, which you'll notice when reviews state something like, "Good work, but everything took longer than expected." Or "Takes forever for him to respond to my messages, but the final work was great."

- Avoid hourly jobs whenever possible. Every project is unique, so that's not always possible, but you'll have fewer issues if you set up each job with a fixed-price for a specific set of tasks. Include a bonus if the time deadlines are met as well.

- Always have every freelancer sign a Non-Disclosure Agreement, no matter how minor or quick the job.

- Don't be tempted to bargain hunt, since like with everything in life, you get what you pay for. In my experience, 90% of the time when a freelancer project doesn't work out it's simply because the hirer went with the cheapest quote. Then they have to hire an expensive freelancer anyway to fix the problem's caused by el Cheapo. It's always cheaper to get things done right the first time. Plus, the marginal costs of paying a few extra bucks an hour for top-tier people is nothing compared to the value you'll receive from above-average performance.

And those costs savings are huge, even if you are paying premium rates to hire a top-quality freelancer. These aren't employees who spend most of their work day on unproductive meetings and busywork. You're only paying for exactly what you need done, and don't have to waste a cent on training, onboarding, health insurance, taxes, et al. Maybe the independent worker is charging $50 a billable hour, but if they can do in eight hours what a $15/hr employee needs 80 clocked office hours for... well, it's fiscally irresponsible not to take advantage of the "gig" economy.

For example, all my companies and various side projects are run with only one full-time employee, but augmented by dozens of special-use freelancers. So I can bring the raw manpower and broad talent set of a major company to bear on a single project, without having to maintain a major payroll year-round.

Legal

Do not underestimate the value of partnering with a great attorney who specializes in *distressed* residential real estate. If you're doing this whole business right, you aren't buying anything on the open market, but rather shopping for deals at auctions and hunting down off-market homes before they hit foreclosure (details in Part 2). Naturally, these properties tend to have all sorts of legal and title risks lurking in the winds, such as multiple mortgages, mechanic/HOA/municipal or other judgement liens, unpaid taxes, absentee landlords, squatters, infinitum ad nauseum. All of which are landmines waiting to blow up your finances… or easy opportunities to unlock extra equity in a home. It all depends on what type of legal representation you arm yourself with before you run into problems.

Sure, for a traditional home purchase, you could hire any random local title agent out of the phonebook to put together the paperwork, but as an investor, you need so much more from your legal rep. You need someone who is used to dealing with these more complicated sales and can sniff out title, debt and zoning troubles before you sign on the bottom line. Even among so-called specialist real estate attorneys, finding one that has verifiable experience with real property development, lien/ foreclosure/ insolvency/ mortgage/ leasing/ brokerage litigation and residential construction law is no simple, "check the block" activity. In short, you should spend more time interviewing lawyers, going over their case history and checking their references than you spend researching your first couple dozen investments.

Remember, the first thing you'll be doing when assuming ownership or even a partial interest in an investment property is to clear the title. Too many investors simply pay off the debts the property owes, but a great lawyer will be able to take the lead and fight/negotiate (two sides of the same coin) on your behalf for a lower payoff, which unlocks far more value in the house than the lawyer's fee cost.

And no agent can help you with this. In fact, licensed Realtors® aren't allowed in their code of ethics to even discuss title issues with their clients, let alone fix them for you and unlock free equity in the home.

Of course, keeping an experienced attorney on retainer is pricey, but many are willing to lower their per sale fees if they're assured of continued repeat business from you. Even more important than shaving a few bucks off your margins is that you want to build a real relationship with your attorney. Trust and understanding are incredibly valuable commodities in any business, and that's doubly true in real estate law. So put some real effort into checking references and past dealings of your title agent, show them your business plan, capital and professionalism... and you just might earn yourself an informal legal partner.

And remember, as soon as you can afford to, bring your favorite attorney onto your team formally, either as a partner or with a long-term retainer. That's the best way to guarantee you get the extra detailed service you need, as well as helping you learn invaluable insights along the way that will make you better at finding equity in investment properties.

Home Inspector

Since you're planning on building a high-volume business and you're planning on remodeling most properties anyway, it might be tempting to save a little cash by skipping the inspection all together. Just. Don't. The inspection is just another aspect of doing your due diligence. You wouldn't buy a property without a detailed title search or sign an unfamiliar contract without your attorney looking it over, so why throw caution to the wind with the physical inspection?

On the same token, don't bother with a discount home inspector who will do the bare-minimum. Like with anything in life, you get what you pay for. The fee for even the most experienced home inspector to perform the most detailed review possible is minuscule compared to the amount of money at stake, yet the potential savings are immense. Plus, there are only three outcomes to a home inspection, all of which are positive for you.

They'll either discover some serious hidden issues that will prompt you to abort the deal and save you a fortune, or find smaller problems that you can use to knock the price down. Even if they find nothing, you can be far more confident in moving ahead with the deal. As an added bonus, a detailed home inspection report can give you some bargaining leverage with contractors that are attempting to exaggerate problems and run up the invoice.

Of course, just because a pro is expensive doesn't mean they're worth the money. You should research their client history and make sure they specialize in the types of properties you're flipping. For example, an inspector who mainly checks condos might miss some key issues with the single-family homes you're flipping.

It's also important to make clear you're seeking a long-term relationship with the inspector. Obviously, any professional is going to give repeat customers more attention.

Home Improvement Contractors

I hear you gritting your teeth already. Finding top notch physical labor that's not only skilled, but also reliable and affordable is an epic challenge in every city. And it's only getting harder as the unemployment rate shrinks. Even if there was a sudden economic downturn, it seems like everyone's going to college nowadays rather than a trade school, so the chronic shortage of quality workers isn't going to end anytime soon.

Personally, I worked around this by partnering with a friend who was already ran a successful construction business. Not just a "handyman" or tradesman, but someone experienced with riding herd on a small army of different specialized contractors. And I mean partnering in a literal, 50/50 equity split arrangement. Partnering with him was more than just a cost-cutting plan, but rather one of the smartest early decisions I made in this business. I bet I would have crashed and burned like so many other new investors instead of thriving without his boundless advice and genuine mentorship. So when I stress the value of seeking out professional advice in everything you do, I'm always speaking from personal experience, since that's how I built our "empire."

On the plus side, remember our goal is just to get properties up to selling condition as soon as possible. Which means you'll save a ton in labor and material costs... assuming you have a reliable partner that can create and coordinate a system for rehabbing the investment before you even buy the property.

Listing Agent

You might be tempted to skip over these people by thinking, "But I am a real estate agent." Or maybe your partner is one. Or perhaps you've been reading the million free resources on the internet about the ins and outs of staging properties for sell. You can get an MLS subscription yourself and naturally, if you follow the pricing strategies outlined in this book, you'll be squeezing out maximum value in each property no matter what. So why do you need someone to negotiate on your behalf and take a huge chunk of your profits?

There are two huge things listing agents can provide you that you can't easily get:

- Local, in-the-trenches information about what property is selling the easiest and what special obstacles you'll be facing in a specific community.

- A ready list of motivated and qualified buyers for that local area.

Best of all, you don't need to formally hire them to work together. There are several ways you both can add value to each other's business. For example, offering a local agent exclusive first showing rights or even a few of the leads you aren't pursuing in exchange for information is win-win for both of you.

Nuts And Bolts –
The Core Math You Need To Work Out
Before Every Deal

The most common reason investors lose money on a house flip isn't because of some sudden change to the local marketplace or a case of bad luck with some random X factor striking out of the blue. Both those risks are easy to manage with a realistic and comprehensive total cost estimate. No, the real cause of investors losing out on the bottom line is because they didn't carefully define that bottom line in the first place.

Most house flippers know better. They understand intellectually that they need to run their retail real estate operation just like any retail business, but they get emotional and lose sight of the bottom line. Yes, it's exhilarating to put in the winning bid on an auction or other off market property for 50% or less off the market price. And if you're in this business, you're likely a secret thrill seeker. I'm guilty of that as well. I love the rush too, but you have to keep yourself grounded and never let those headline numbers cloud your judgment. If you're not acting as a cold-hearted calculator, then you're not really an investor; you're just a gambler with a fancy title.

But if you want to create real value that buyers will pay a premium for, the first and most important step is real simple: don't buy crappy properties just because they're cheap.

The ideal flipping candidate requires only routine "wear and tear" repair, so you can pour most of your budget into renovating and creating new value, rather than wasting funds getting the house into a habitable condition first.

Remember, we're after opportunities to create equity, and dirt-cheap properties make that process far harder. First, they tend to have serious problems, such as expensive, non-negotiable liens or expansive repairs you need to fix before you can even start adding value. Second, there's more guesswork needed on the estimated costs for these fixer-uppers, which increases the risk you'll underestimate the costs. Which is pretty much the exact opposite of managing risk.

As for me, I find the 70% rule too vague. It's a good, conservative rule of thumb when you're starting out and aren't that confident in your ability to accurately predicate costs and home values, but for lasting success you need to be more specific. I narrow down the margins of error by comparing the current equity to *realistic* estimates of all my costs (renovation, repairs, staging, holding, closing) and the hype-free market value of the home. By the way, determining these realistic numbers is where choosing your niche and sticking to certain types of properties, locations, etc really pays off, but more on that in the next chapter.

Once I have this estimate for every potential property in my target area on one spreadsheet, I can compare prospects and decide which homes are worth contacting the owner about. I usually won't even consider making an offer unless I'm sure there's at least 25% equity already locked in immediately. Meaning there's a 25% spread between the sum of my purchase price and estimated total costs, and the realistic price I can fetch on the open market within four months. In some rare cases I might pull the trigger with as little as 15% equity, but only if it's a particularly hot market where properties are moving extra fast.

Time is THE key variable of your pricing and valuation system

Which leads me to a crucial point that most people gloss over when discussing market value and pricing strategies. Time is not just a factor in the process, but the single most critical variable. Yes, yes, everyone knows that "time is money" … but exactly how much money is time worth? Once you calculate the giant leap in profits from selling fast into your bottom line, or the heavy cost of slow inventory turnover, you'll never look at home pricing the same way again.

Unless you're planning on renting properties and speculating on long-term capital appreciation, how fast you can lock in a profit is more valuable than how much profit you make. I know I'm a broken record, but the safest and most lucrative strategy is to flip properties every four months. Even faster would be ideal, but there are still real-world delays with closing that slow down even the hottest markets. So four months, from initial purchase to signing over title, is the target goal for three reasons:

1) Maximizing profit.

You don't even need a calculator to whistle at the mind-blowing effects of compound interest at play here. Each sale you close allows you to invest more into the next deal, or even better, multiple investments at once. Earning a little, but doing it often increases your potential earnings exponentially. Every home you buy ties up capital, while everyone you sell frees up capital. It's all about the size of your inventory, how fast you can offload them and how long it takes to build more inventory. Which is why pros don't stress over the final sale price much, but worry about every minute their cash is tied up in a property.

For example, say you have the option to flip a place immediately for only 15% profit, or maybe you could earn 50% on a property if you took all year to renovate it or you priced on the high end of the home value and refused to take a lower offer. If you move it fast, then you'll free up enough cash to flip two similar homes in the next investing round instead of just one. Even if you only net the same 15% on both of these sales, a rather conservative estimate, you'll build up your working capital enough to flip *four* houses the next time. So we're at seven flips in a single year. Sure, the per unit profit was only modest, but the net returns for the year will be double or more what you would have earned sitting on a single property and trying to eke out every last cent.

2) Minimizing risk.

If no single good investment can make your career, no single disaster can break your business. You'll hear me constantly driving this point home, because only constant repetition can drown out the greedy, animalistic part of our brains that wants to throw caution to the wind and score "the big dirty." The oft-repeated risk management strategy of "diversifying your portfolio" doesn't mean trying out a bunch of different things. It just means decentralizing your sources of income, and therefore the potential impact of any source of risk. By all means, trade the type of properties you're most comfortable with and know the most about. Just trade as many as you can instead of putting all your eggs in one basket.

3) Speed builds confidence, skill, reputation and relationships.

All the investment books in the world won't teach you as much as you'll learn from actually conducting a flip yourself. And the more practice you have, the more deals you close, the more unteachable lessons you'll learn. Which ensures you're wiser, savvier and more confident on your next investments.

In the process, you'll be earning a reputation in your local market, which will make lead generation and finding hidden discounts even easier. Just as in important, the more deals you close, the deeper the relationships you'll build with advisers, contractors, lawyers, inspectors, appraisers, lenders, agents and all the other facilitators in your industry. That alone will reap boundless rewards for years to come as you learn from the best specialists in each field, as well as affording you professional favors the average investor could only dream about.

Keeping Track of Estimated Equity

Throughout this investment process you'll have to decide on many different forks in the road. For example:

- Should you accept a buy offer that's X% less than your asking, but you can close Y months faster than expected?

- You get multiple offers with different terms. One is willing to pay a higher price, but needs you to pay cash up front to cover their closing costs. The other is a slightly lower price, but they buyer needs no other help. Which one is the best deal for you?

- Rental rates in a neighborhood you planned to flip a property in are higher than you expected, and the mortgage lender seems quite amenable to a short payoff. How long would you need to rent the property to unlock the same equity as a regular sale?

In each case you'll have to update your estimated equity score to compare the end result of multiple courses of action. The best way to do this is to treat the equity changes in hypothetical scenarios as costs or surplus, instead of increases/reductions to equity. Then you compare the different plans against the status quo estimated equity. To avoid confusion or "corrupting" this all-important equity estimate, make sure you always have just one "mother" equity score at a time.

Estimating Your Total Costs

So there you are, on the phone with a downtrodden home owner who's clearly desperate to make a deal before the sheriff shows up with an eviction notice. You place your all cash offer and take a deep breath as the phone goes silent. You've done some careful research on the title and neighborhood, even sent a home inspector and did a physical walkthrough yourself.

You're absolutely confident that with some small tweaks, you can add some serious value and sell this home for at least 200k within 90 days. You're plugging different contractor quotes into an Excel spreadsheet to see which improvement options give the most bang for your buck when the homeowner finally says something.

"Fine," she murmurs over her husband cussing in the background. "It doesn't leave us much after we pay off the mortgage, but I guess we'll take your deal. Assuming you can get the cash here today."

"No problem, ma'am. We'll take this mess off your hands today. I'm on my way to the bank right now."

You hang up and snatch your car keys, ignoring your half-finished cost estimate. Ah, what difference does it make? You just landed a

200k off-market house for only 165k after acquisition and final payoff costs! Renovations will cost 5-10k, the title is clear and you're dealing in all-cash, so no financing costs; the petty details can't change the big picture. Even if there are some small surprises, you'll still come out well ahead, right? How could anything go wrong?

But you're no longer clapping yourself on the back months later when you offload the house and grit your teeth at the cost spreadsheet you only just now finished. If you'd only taken five more minutes to fill this out way back when...

Sure enough, you sold the place at $200k, but where did all the equity go? Instead of deducting only $165k for the house and paying off the mortgage, plus your top estimate of $10k more in renovations, somehow you actually took a loss. How the heck did that happen? So you pour over the expenditures line by line to see what you missed, only to learn just how big the devil was hiding in the details.

First, you forgot all about the upfront closing costs on both ends of the flip. Thanks to that darn new tax levy, document fees are much higher than last year. So that's $5,000 in cash you had to shell out.

Oh, and of course, at the last second a pending lien for unpaid homeowner association dues was approved and added to the title, so out goes an extra $2,000 to make that problem go away.

Also, thanks to a sudden revision to the local water management district's risk assessment, the house is now in a designated flood zone. Your insurance costs triple, but that's okay, since you're going to sell fast...

But then there was that problem the contractors found. Thankfully you added a little wiggle room to the renovation budget, so the total cost wasn't a game changer... but it took them two extra months to complete the project. So there goes another $5,000 up in smoke thanks to your increased holding costs.

Oh yeah, and that air conditioner the home inspector warned you was on its last leg? Sure enough, it broke down during this extra time you were stuck holding the property. So instead of the home warranty paying for it, or you having time to shop around for a good deal on a new unit, you're now on the hook for a hasty $3,000 replacement.

Since you held on to the place so long, you then needed some serious landscaping work to get rid of all the weeds and make the place presentable. And where the heck did this broken window come from? Must be those darn teenagers always hanging around. Go ahead and dump another $1,000 out in hasty maintenance work.

At this point, you just want to get this thing off your hands and move on to another project. You've lost count of how many opportunities you've missed out on in these five months, so you hire a top-notch real estate agent to close a deal in a hurry, despite originally planning to skip an agent and do things yourself. They find you a motivated buyer real fast that's ready to pay the listing price, but this service cost another 5%, so there goes $10,000.

Then, at the last moment, your buyer ran into a liquidity problem after his lender demanded a couple of extra home appraisals and other inspections. So you dug into your thin pockets again and covered his remaining $2,000 closing costs to keep the deal from falling through and make sure you didn't have to go with a backup offer below the listing price.

So when everything was said and done, all those "little" details added together raised your total costs to $38,000. Even though you were spot-on about the cost of renovations and how much value you could add, you still came away with a net loss of $3,000.

If you'd only created a comprehensive total cost estimate first, you could have set your maximum purchase price at $150,000 and still have come out with a $12,000 profit, even with all these nasty surprises.

But how exactly do you create a realistic and detailed total cost estimate?

First, the prep work to simplify things. If you haven't done so already, separate your rental and your flipping activities. Not just didn't accounting ledgers, but they should also be two separate legal entities. Also separate your fixed operating costs that you're going to pay anyway to stay in business, such as technical subscription services and assistants, from your variable costs involved with each investment.

Now you can estimate your expected costs, both direct and indirect, and subtract it from the property's equity before you get started. Now this is a dynamic process, starting with initial estimates and refining as new information comes in, but it's not particularly time consuming.

Most of this is actually common sense, but the biggest key is to make sure you factor in enough time. For example, if you're flipping a property, then with every recurring cost you should initially budget for six months of expenses. Then refine that later when you have pending sales data of how long similar homes stayed on the market. Then refine yet again when you're on market and evaluating different offers that come in ahead of the budget.

Before you make any investment, you want to total up the expected costs from entering and exiting position, rehabbing and then holding. We'll go into the step by step details of how to find all this data later, but here's your basic checklist for all three phases.

Acquisition and Closing Costs

For an investor, closing costs when we enter a position and exit one are calculated a little differently than your typical home buyer/seller. Some of these expenses aren't traditional closing costs, so they're usually tossed in the "miscellaneous" accounting category. This can really throw off your initial equity estimate and lead to all sorts of unwelcome surprises down the road. The simplest way to make sure you aren't missing anything is to roll all these items into two categories:

1) Total acquisition costs: This is the sum total of everything it costs to enter the investment, regardless of the property source or your long-term strategy.

- Amount paid at auction

- Amount paid to homeowner

- Eviction costs

- All legal costs for document prep/filing, in addition to the standard recording title transfer fees. If your legal service isn't in house, these constant little $25, $50, $100 mosquito bites can add up fast and bleed out a ton of equity.

- Traditional closings costs, such as inspections, agent commission, title search, document stamp, etc...

2) Total unloading costs: This is really different for two reasons. First, you need to pay attention to the difference between costs out of your pocket and increases/reductions to your available equity. For example, say your estimated equity was based upon taking six months to sell the house, but it took eight months to close. That reduction in your equity, in the form of a higher mortgage payoff amount, should be calculated as a closing cost even though you're not paying anything directly. That will make it much easier to compare and contrast different offers on the property, since you'll have only one estimated equity value that you can then compare to each course of action (offer). Sounds like a small accounting detail, but having more than one equity score gets confusing in a hurry.

The second issue is that time plays a big role if you purchased a property under foreclosure and want to use the new buyer's funds to pay off the mortgage instead of your own. Here, calculating a final loan payoff isn't as simple as closing out a traditional home sell. The mortgage owner will push for an inflated settlement that includes late fees, extra interest and enough attorney fees to cover a celebrity trial. In many cases, you can negotiate this settlement down, but the longer it takes to close, the less leverage you'll have. For every extra month it takes you to close, you can expect 1-2% in extra charges from the foreclosing lender.

- Final settlement for all lien holders
- Any credits/financial considerations given to buyer to expediate the sale.
- Traditional closing costs, such as agent fees, transfer taxes title insurance, home seller insurance, etc...

Note: If you accepted an offer for a lower price than your listing, that isn't counted here. That's deducted from the estimated equity before you start adding closing costs.

Rehabbing costs

This is the catchall category for everything needed to get the property in a marketable and sellable state, both physically and in terms of title. This goes beyond just basic repair and renovation costs. You want to include:

- All physical labor and materials costs for repairs and renovations.

- Permitting, inspection and code violation costs for any renovation you've done or the previous owners have done. This is too often overlooked and causes nasty surprises when you're ready to sell.

- All staging costs beyond renovations, such as cleaning services, landscaping, pressure washing, etc…

- Costs to clear out smaller liens that you aren't covering in closing costs, such as HOA and unpaid property taxes.

- In addition, set aside an additional 10% of the total rehab cost for surprise maintenance or other unknowns.

Holding costs

Even if you're purchasing properties in cash to resell fast, your holding costs are not an inconsequently thing. These costs also come in quite handy when deciding if a low-ball but fast offer for your property is worth it or not.

- Utility costs.

- Recurring HOA dues.

- Insurance.

- Property management fees. If you're not using a 3rd party management firm, this includes everything needed to keep the property in pristine condition, such as security monitoring and regular landscape maintenance.

Liquidity

In addition to how much you're investing, it's crucial to work out how much free cash you'll need during each stage of the operation, including a healthy safety margin. If you don't have the necessary funds in reserve already and you're relying on future cash flow from somewhere else, make sure you have a backup option in case some X factor affects your finances. This could be as simple as an unused line of credit with your bank or pre-qualifying for a working capital loan.

Obviously for maximum profit and minimum risk, any form of debt financing should be used as a last resort. However, once you've purchased a property and some unexpected crisis pops up, even something totally unrelated to the home in question, it would be a shame to blow a six-figure deal just because you're shy a grand or two for hasty repairs or unexpected legal fees that have to be paid for immediately.

So make sure you have at least a working capital line of credit option available from your bank for emergencies. Despite the high interest rates, that's usually far cheaper than offering a buyer big credits against the price, or even scuttling the deal altogether.

Cash Talks, BS Walks –
Why Cash Is King And Financing Makes
You A Pawn

One of the hardest things for new investors to grasp is the need to stick with all cash deals. You might think I'm some type of overly cautious Scrooge McDuck trying to scare off cash poor new investors by screaming about the "evils of credit." It might even sound hypocritical of me, since I've used leverage to great effect early in my career.

But the reality is that even a small stack of cash opens up all sorts of opportunities that are closed to you if you're chained to debt. On the plus side, using just cash for new investments doesn't mean you need a mountain of money on hand though. I can, and have routinely, made more money with just a $10,000 cashier's check working the pre-foreclosure or HOA foreclosure auctions than I could with a $200,000 bank loan to go after on-market listings. Unless you're operating in an ultra-hot marketplace, it's rare you'll ever spend more than $100,000 upfront on a single deal.

Even if you're planning on doing mainly long-term rentals and would rather risk the bank's money instead of your own, financing is still fraught with additional risk. Times are changing and what worked in the early years of the housing crisis is a much costlier strategy today. Back when the Federal Reserve slashed rates to nothing and banks were giving away practically "free money," with even short-term mortgage interest rates just slightly above inflation, then purchasing your investments with as little cash down as possible was a smart move.

Today though, and for the foreseeable future, things are radically different. Not only are interest rates rising, but the requirements to secure financing are tightening, especially for new investors. Most of all, the key is risk management. Yes, you're risking your own cash in off-market deals, but only the title transfer, initial rehab and holding costs. All the big-ticket expenses, like paying off the mortgage, are paid at closing. Really, financed by your buyer. If you've done your homework, then the risk is limited because you built in a generous equity cushion before entering the deal. The worst that can happen is that you miscalculated your costs or sales price and wind up taking a smaller profit than expected.

However, when you're financing a deal, are you really any safer? You must be purchasing at market rates, or quite close, to secure a loan in the first place. Think about the additional risks that complicate your investment formula:

a. You're giving up the massive equity safety margin that protects you from mistakes.

b. You're still paying off the existing mortgage from your own pocket, instead of letting your eventual buyer pay it. In essence, you're just swapping one loan for another.

c. Nowadays, your down payment will likely be so large that it rivals the cost of just buying in cash at auction or approaching the homeowner with a title transfer deal.

d. You're giving up all flexibility when purchasing the deal. I can't recall how many times I've seen an investor work out a great deal, but in the weeks while they're waiting for the bank's underwriters to finish the details, an all-cash investor swoops in first.

Cash Unlocks Better Deals.

But more important than just the slightly higher costs of financing is your lack of flexibility. Whether you plan to found a long-term rental empire or master high-velocity house flipping, you need to be able to strike fast. When you've found a distressed home owner with serious equity in their home who's ready to sale fast for a song, the last thing you need is to be waiting on some bank's underwriters to triple check your loan application. The homeowner you went to so much trouble to find and warm up will probably receive a dozen cash-offers from more nimble investors before your bank even sends out a property appraiser.

I've lost count of how many times I've approached homeowners in a desperate situation and knocked 50% or more off an already reduced asking price just by sticking a certified cashier's check in their hands.

But using hard cash to secure better deals is table stakes in this game. The real value of skipping lenders and using only cash is in the incredible flexibility it gives you. You can snap up lucrative but fleeting chances in a heartbeat or jump ship with minimum damage even if you bought the worst money pit.

In those same situations where I'm talking to homeowners directly, mine is rarely the first offer that's come their way. In fact, I'm always the lowest bidder, even when competing with other house flippers, yet I'm still closing the deal 90% of the time.

Sure, I like to think that's solely because of my charming *je ne sais quoi*... but if I'm being honest, it's simply because I deal in all cash, all the time. Never underestimate the seductive power of an "offensive" low ball cash offer, when delivered at the right time, with sympathy and understanding. When you're dealing with a person teetering on the abyss of financial ruin, a poor soul drowning in the emotional turmoil of how to keep food in their kids' mouths and a roof over their heads... well, the small life ring you're tossing out right now is infinitely more valuable than the promise of a rescue boat next week.

Your offer to make all their problems go away right now, before lunchtime, and buy this financial albatross "as is" makes you saving angel. All those other offers requiring some lender's approval days or weeks down the road, no matter how much more they're worth, are just empty promises when stacked against a pile of cash in a desperate person's hands.

Find Your Niche –
The Big Fish In A Little Pond Is Always
Fat And Happy

So precisely how can the John or Jane Doe average investor compete with the multi-billion dollar investment firms, REITs and tech giants prowling the markets for quick flips? This task is not as daunting as it seems, because the sheer nationwide size of these giants is their Achilles heel.

No one can buy everything, not even the filthy rich, so these firms intentionally ignore millions of good opportunities every day by focusing on the best potential deals in their niche. Their prime area of expertise. That focus is what gives them an edge… and you a template for success.

Whether you're flipping homes, founding a rental empire or just looking to scoop up and settle liens, you need some edge for lasting success. Yes, yes, that's what everyone says, but they never follow through and explain *how*. It's really quite simple. Your edge is the niche you choose to focus on. That's it. Simply concentrating all your energy on one goal at a time gives you an advantage over the competition who are trying to do everything at once.

For example, if you focus on flipping auction sales of condos in a single section of a city, you'll already have a leg up on those flipping condos city wide even if you're just starting out. The more narrow niches you can add value to, the greater your edge.

As for me, I know my limitations and strengths. I'm a numbers and research guy, but if you give me a hammer, I'll wind up somehow setting the place on fire. That's why I have a great partner who brings huge value through his expertise at all types of construction and handling contractors. He knows all the tricks and lingo, so he keeps the physical work on schedule and done right, while squeezing the subcontractors for their best prices.

While he's squaring away the nitty gritty details of rehab, renovation and maintenance, I focus all my energy into my niches:

1. Data mining *Lis Pendens* and other public records for troubled properties with high equity.

2. Tracking down the owner and tossing them a well-crafted cash offer lifeline before the sharks swallow them up.

3. Then grab my legal speargun and drive the sharks away so we can salvage the sinking treasure ship in peace.

Together, we've made a team that's dominated our local market for years, while adding new niche members to the organization that gives us even more of an edge.

For example, we've also partnered with an attorney who can run circles around competing lien holders. Those unfocused bank lawyers look like terrified tuna when my great white shark of a lawyer rolls up, since her niche is focusing 100% on the winner-take-all type of legal warfare we need.

You can build your own edge out of nothing just by breaking down the retail real estate investment process into its simplest components, and then choosing those areas that you have some experience with, even if only rudimentary, to focus all your time and effort on. That's all a niche is—focus. If you're concentrating on a single aspect of each part of the flipping process, you will become an expert in short order.

For the maximum edge, I'd recommend choosing one niche from each category and then pour all your energy into learning more about each field. Again, you don't have to be an expert already, but just have some basic familiarity with the subject matter, a desire to learn more and the discipline to study hard.

✓ WHO are you selling to?

End user niches, such as long/short term rentals, student rentals, etc...

✓ WHAT are you flipping?

Property niches, such as single-family houses, condos, etc...

66

✓ WHERE will you focus your searches?

Location niches, specific city/region plus specialty like suburbs, downtown, etc…

✓ WHEN will you consider buying a property or property interest?

Seller niches, such as auctions, pre-foreclosures, assignment of rights, etc…

✓ HOW will you do things differently than the competition?

Investor skill niches, such as data mining, renovating, staging properties, etc…

You may be a "small fry" investor now, but if you're at least trying to master one niche in each of these fields of study, then you are the definition of a true professional. Choosing your own niche also helps you get maximum value out of hiring investment advisors, since you can narrow down the scope of questions you have and receive far more detailed advice.

While it's impossible to discuss every possible niche in this business in one book (or even a dozen), I want to give a quick overview of some popular niches that are easiest to dominate. The low hanging fruit that have the shortest learning curves and fewest obstacles in the way of mastering them. Once you've chosen an answer to those who, what, where, when and how questions to focus on, then you'll have a foundation we can build upon when we tackle the much more complicated but all-important niche of finding high value off-market properties.

Who – End user niches

Buyer Types

Obviously, no home is a perfect fit for everyone. So by narrowing your focus to selecting, renovating and marketing homes for a particular type of homebuyer, you can increase the speed that you turn over inventory as well as unlock additional value. I'm not suggesting extensive customization when you rehab a property, but simply understanding the needs and desires of a type of buyer who would be attracted to a property gives you a big leg up on the competition.

In the broadest sense, all potential buyers can be divided into retail or investor purchasers. When selling to investors (wholesaling), if you can identify what unique edge your property will provide, you can stress those advantages and close deals faster. For example, rental focused buy-and-let investors are looking for recently renovated homes that are move-in ready and extremely low-maintenance. Speculative investors would want to see how this property has a good chance of appreciating in value faster than the other homes in the neighborhood. Other house flippers want to see homes that are discounted deeply for their poor condition so they can fix them up.

With retail buyers, you have even more opportunities to stand out from the pack. For some examples, a small and older house in a quiet neighborhood is likely a better fit for retired buyers than first time homeowners. Families are looking for space, safety and good school districts and less interested in specific amenities. Young childish couples looking for a starter home are usually more interested in proximity to popular destinations and how vibrant the community is, rather than a large yard. The list goes on and on. The key thing is that no home is perfect for every buyer, so to close fast and at the best price, you need to know who your ideal buyer is before you even list the property.

I'm of course a huge advocate of flipping as fast as possible to maximize profit and minimize risk, but I have rented out all sorts of single and multi-family units over the years. I understand the value a savvy investor can create if they focus on rentals, especially in markets where rents are rising faster than home prices. So let's explore the easiest rental niches you could dominate in a hurry if you choose to.

Rentals – Both Long & Short Term

Earning steady and semi-passive rental income is just about everyone's dream investment... which is why this niche is so darn crowded. However, when you're bringing offline properties to the market, none of that competition means anything to you. The whole equation of finding the perfect location that will attract quality tenants and keep them there is flipped on its head when you can take properties that have never been rented out onto the market in the first place.

If you're dreaming of setting up a network of Airbnb style short-term rentals in hot vacation areas, like so many nowadays, then this niche is still easy to break into. Just refine your web scrapers to pull Lis Pendens or Notice of Defaults from your favorite locales around the country and you're already well ahead of the game.

Specialty User Rentals

This niche has many different sub-genres, depending on your stomping grounds. If you're investing in a college town, then you might want to focus on student housing. Which usually means renovating to reduce common areas and maximizing the number of bedrooms.

If you're investing location is near a beach or other popular holiday spot, you probably want to focus on vacation rentals, with an emphasize on view and access to amenities. Even if you're focusing on a less than affluent section of a major city, you can specialize in helping tenants navigate the bureaucracy and paperwork to attain Section 8 or other government housing vouchers.

Lease-To-Own

If you're planning on renting out the property, or circumstances force your hand, an increasing popular option are lease-to-own arrangements. All of the terms are flexible, but in broad strokes the renter pays a lump sum amount, usually between 2-5% of the home's value, for the right to purchase the home at a fixed price, usually above current market value, within a certain time frame, often 12-18 months. The owner keeps the option payment regardless if the renter purchases the property or not.

In addition, the renter's monthly rent is usually higher than the property would normally command, but a portion is credited to the home's final sale price if the leaser purchases the house. These agreements can be structured to provide maximum flexibility to the homebuyer and allow them to purchase a property they couldn't otherwise afford, while securing the investor an immediate high-quality tenant, modest quick payout and a larger potential profit over time.

This is a niche best served by those with a particular interest in the legal technicalities behind the contracts, as well as investors able to carefully screen tenant-leasers. When executed right though, the short and long-term benefits are significant for buy-and-let investors. While not right for everyone, especially if you want to flip fast or expect local property values or rent rates to rise soon, these contracts offer additional options to carve out your own niche.

What – Property niches

Single Family Houses

Advantages

- High demand – Single family houses represent roughly 60% of US housing inventory for a good reason: they're in high demand in most markets. That's why these homes are generally the fastest to flip, assuming the price isn't too high for the neighborhood.

- Capital appreciation – As a general rule, I don't advocate betting on housing prices to rise. Speculating is a hard business model to sustain long-term, but if prices do increase in your market, more often than not nationwide single-family homes appreciate in value much faster than any other residential property type.

Challenges

- Valuation – Unless the home is smack in the middle of a cookie-cutter subdivision, you'll need to put in some extra work to create your own list of realistic "comp" sales. Bear in mind that even the most well-researched comparative market analysis will have a large margin of error when dealing with single family homes. So if you're pricing on the high end of your valuation estimate, don't be surprised if closing takes longer than usual, for example when the buyer's lender requires an extra appraisal or the underwriters drag their feet.

- Holding costs – If you're planning on extensive remodeling, wind up pricing too high or some other issue keeps you from selling this home fast, your holding costs will be higher than properties at similar prices. For example, multi-unit properties allow you to rent out part of the property to offset your costs and condos don't usually require such high landscaping, maintenance and insurance costs as single-family homes. So making sure you have the right estimates and a system in place to make a fast exit are major factors to turn a profit with these types of homes.

Manufactured Homes

Possible Areas of Focus

Neighborhood – Compared to single and multi-family homes, the immediate neighborhood has a much more profound impact on a manufactured home's curb appeal. The fanciest triple-wide in a rundown, crime infested trailer park won't fetch nearly the same price as an older single-wide on its own plot in a "respectable" neighborhood. So to succeed with these types of properties, you need a deep-dive understanding of the area and the people that live there.

Advantages

Rate of return – For a niche flipper who focuses on these types of properties and knows how to manage the risks, you'll find that no other type of property offers so much potential gain for so little an initial investment. For example, the same capital investment you would usually put into a single traditional home will likely purchase two or more relatively new manufactured homes. Each of which should net you 15-30%, if you've done your homework right.

More distressed owner opportunities – At the risk of sounding callous, a higher percentage of manufactured homes in most markets will wind up in foreclosure proceedings. Since many of the biggest real estate investment players don't bother with these types of properties, you can shop around a wider selection of distressed homeowners to find those with equity and make an ultra-low cash offer with less competition.

Challenges

Depreciation – Generally, manufactured homes lose value every year faster than a "stick built" home will. This varies massively by market, but 3-5% depreciation every year for the structure is a common metric. Of course, this doesn't necessarily spell disaster, since just like other properties the land can appreciate in value, the neighborhood's overall property values could rise from a supply/demand imbalance, plus certain renovations can add enough value to overcome for the property's depreciation. However, flipping manufactured homes does require an excellent grasp of local market values and an insight into the desires of the end users purchasing or renting these homes.

Lower demand – While no other type of home offers a better price per square foot rate, and the quality of modern manufactured homes is outstanding, nonetheless many home buyers are just not interested in these types of properties, regardless of price. And compared to other home buyer categories, you'll find a smaller percentage of those interested in manufactured homes are actually qualified prospects (able to qualify for a mortgage fast). So expect these types of homes to stay on the market longer than other properties.

Financing – Even when you can find qualified buyers, these homes are much harder for them to finance than other options. Some lenders don't even cover manufactured homes and those that do tend to require better credit histories or charge higher interest rates from the borrowers. In some cases, such as with FHA loans, the maximum loan amount for mobile/manufactured homes is capped at a single amount nationwide, which might not cover the price of the home and land in your locale.

Multi-Family Housing

Advantages

Rental opportunities – Whether duplexes, triplexes or quads, these homes combine the valuation advantages of single lot homes with multiple units you can rent out for a steady income stream. Even if renting isn't your long-term strategy, even short-term rentals on some units while you're renovating others will substantially reduce your holding costs, and could even generate a positive cash flow.

Larger buyer pool – Unlike with other properties, multi-family housing offers you different exit strategies. You'll attract attention across a broader selection of homebuyers, from new families looking for a starter home, singles wanting their own place to commercial investors looking to buy a long-term cash cow. And in the meantime, you can lease some units while waiting for the best offer.

Where – Location niches

As a retail residential investor, nothing gives you a bigger advantage over the nationwide real estate "pros" than being intimately familiar with a particular location. Your gut instincts into what people are looking for in a local area, the vibe of a community, the amenities that are in high demand, et al constitutes a treasure trove of data that gives you a competitive edge.

With that said, the more narrowly you define your "stomping grounds," the stronger that edge will be. Many new investors will arbitrarily set their investment zone within a certain drive distance, usually an hour or so, from their own home. While practical and convenient, it's far better to identify the locales you want to focus on, no matter how far away they are. Study the regions/cities and subzones within that have the most homes matching your other skills/interests and ignore everything else.

When you're just starting out, I'd strongly recommend focusing on flipping off-market properties in just one of the following narrowly defined locations. Once you're quite comfortable with your chosen niche, then expand and experiment with other location types.

Focus on School Districts, Community Activities, & Amenities

An alternative to flipping in a popular, and likely overpriced neighborhood, is to focus on the features that make the area so popular. For example, if everyone wants to live near some hip park or send their kids to a particular school, you might want to skip the hoity-toity new development within sight of the place. Just searching a little farther afield will usually yield neighborhoods within a reasonable distance that aren't hyped up and have more reasonable prices.

Big or small, every town has other less obvious hotspots that run up the local property values, such as greenways, public spaces, commercial centers, centers of nightlife, and other amenities.

Quite often, many homebuyers are just looking for a "status" address, such as one in a rich township or classy suburb of a city. If you can offer them a cheaper housing alternative just outside of the high-class areas, but yet close enough that the post office still labels it "Fancy Town, USA," you'll unlock even more value in your investment.

When – Seller niches

Pre-Foreclosure/Short Sales

This niche has countless sub-categories you could specialize in, but they all boil down to finding and approaching homeowners that are behind on their payments and facing impending foreclosure, but still have equity in their property.

Naturally, the period between a *Lis Pendens* being filed and the start of an auction is a great time for an angel investor to swoop in and save a motivated seller from the hassle, cost, and embarrassment of a foreclosure.

But that's only the beginning. The mortgage lender is usually just as motivated to avoid the trouble and risk of foreclosing and auctioning off assets, so they're often quite amenable to all-cash short sale offers at this time. Especially if the party suing for foreclosure is not a top priority creditor, such as a home owner's association or HELOC lender, since their risk exposure is so high. Not to mention the other opportunities you'll find to gain interest, deed or other rights assignments to a property for a song, but we'll cover all that in the next chapter.

Estates/Probates

A unique class of off-market homes with motivated sellers are the heirs of recently deceased property owners. In these emotional times, the families tend to place a priority on liquidating and distributing the estate's assets as fast as possible. Sometimes for financial reasons, sometimes to find closure or avoid internal strife in the family. In any case, selling the home fast with minimum hassle is almost as important as the price.

Yet at the same time, these homes are usually far from ready to sell. Faced with the expense and delay of properly staging a home and finding a local agent, all while the new estate owners tend to live a long distance away, they will often jump at the chance to take a low but immediate cash offer to make the headache go away.

The biggest downside is naturally all the potential stakeholders that need to sign off on a sale. Which can also be an advantage, since the extra time it takes to close scares off so many professional investors.

Divorce

Similar to estate sales, quite often joint real property needs to be liquidated in a hurry during divorce proceedings. Investors with high emotional intelligence, for example, can navigate this emotional battlefield and arrange win-win deals for themselves and the estranged homeowners well before the property comes to market. As an added bonus, in many states the initial petition to divorce is a matter of public record, so you can jump on these deals fast while facing much less competition from other cash investors.

Damaged properties

While often overlooked, purchasing properties recently damaged by fires, flooding or other disasters can be a lucrative niche for flippers whose strong suit is construction and renovation. Quite often the owners would prefer to take their insurance settlement and move on to another home rather than face the emotional and financial trouble of rebuilding. So you can often purchase these properties at "salvage" rates and unlock massive value when you rebuild. Again, this is more of an advanced niche, but worth mentioning for those of you with an edge in construction infrastructure and contacts.

HOA, tax delinquencies and other junior liens

While every state has a slightly different procedure, an investor focusing on just lien speculating in a single market will have a huge advantage over the competition. This is such a wide-open niche with ample exit strategies that allows you to purchase deeds, interest in a property or rights assignments, all before, during, and after an auction.

How – Investor Skill niches

While there are countless investor skills you can hone, we'll cover the biggest ones that will pay off no matter what other niches you're focusing on:

- Data Mining
- Staging
- Renovation
- Legal
- Lead generation

PHASE TWO:
Bringing It All Together

Best Sources Of Flipping & Rental Opportunities – Off Market Is The Only Market

I know I'm beating this dead horse well into the afterlife, but I can't stress this point enough. The most common source of failure in this business is trying to invest in properties that are already for sale on the open market. Eventually you'll sell through the MLS, but don't ever shop from it. If you're cruising the internet and looking for some "sucker" you can lowball... well, then you're the sucker that's going to get ripped off.

These homes are priced too close to market value, if not overvalued, so good luck finding that 25% built-in equity you'll need to still turn a profit after closing and holding costs. Even if the seller made a mistake and undervalued their property, or they're ultra-motivated and willing to negotiate, the competition for these so-called "deals" is far too stiff, and you'll have no advantage over all the other players. In the unlikely event you beat the odds by winning the bidding war and still turn a profit, it'll be a one-off event. Not the type of reproduceable strategy you can replicate endlessly and scale up to build a reliable business from.

Take emotion out of the equation. I've heard even some professionals say you should only buy homes for investment that you would like to live in. Such advice leaves me scratching my head. Besides the obvious fact that your decision to purchase should be 100% determined by the underlying numbers, the types of properties you can flip fast tend to be fairly blasé housing units that have mass market appeal.

But no matter what you do, never forget the only real hunting grounds for equity are found at foreclosure auctions and when dealing directly with distressed homeowners. If you stick to that principle and run your equity estimates carefully, it's hard *not* to make money any market.

Foreclosure Process And Opportunities

Since you're not going to find significant equity in homes already for sale on the market, then we will be dealing with properties that are at some stage of the pre-foreclosure process. You don't have to be a foreclosure specialist at the beginning to take advantage of the system, although you will reach that skill level faster than you might think. In the meantime, lean on your attorney to cover all the legal minutia. Make them earn their keep.

Right now, you just need to focus on mastering the "big picture" of how all these moving parts fit together and where you can step in to add value. In the next phase we'll bring all these strategies together in step by step practice.

There are two main types of lender-originated foreclosures, but both lead to the same goal of selling the home to pay off the outstanding debt, the vast majority of the time through a public auction. Now, I focus the most attention on judicial foreclosures throughout this book, since they offer several unique advantages for investors. Still, most of these strategies, tips, tricks, as well as notes of caution, can be applied to evaluate equity, unlock new value and gain a competitive advantage in non-judicial foreclosures.

Now, the state you're operating in does play a major role on your investment strategy. Not your success or failure rate, of course not, but how aggressively you should pursue certain options. For example, Florida requires that all foreclosures must be judicial, where the lender sues the borrower to go to auction. In this case, gaining title from the homeowner and then delaying the sale while you flip the property or earn a rental income in the meantime are fairly simple and lucrative strategies.

On the other hand, California requires that all foreclosures be non-judicial, where the lender can go straight to auction by following a public notice procedure. Since it's harder and more expensive to delay a sale there, it's usually a better strategy to focus on negotiating cash-for-keys settlements with the lender or positioning yourself as the surplus holder when the property goes to auction so you have bidding leverage.

Complicating things further, many states allow both foreclosure types without mandating one or the other, letting the borrower and lender decide the terms of the mortgage contract. Quite often this includes adding special failure to pay provisions to the contract, which may or may not even hold up in court. *Sigh*. I know, but I warned you'd be spending a ton of time talking to your lawyer. Don't worry though. When you understand the broad strokes and the opportunities available with each foreclosure, you'll know exactly what questions to ask your attorney. That alone puts you way ahead of most of your competitors.

Judicial Foreclosure

This is where the mortgage owner files a civil lawsuit against the original borrower to recover the unpaid debt by forcing a sale of the property. There are procedural differences in each state, such as length of redemption periods, time between notices and extra paperwork, but the general process works like this:

1) *Notice.* After 4-6 months of missed payments, the lender files a Lis Pendens (generic notice of lawsuit) at the county courthouse where the property is located. This is all a matter of public record, since it serves to warn perspective buyers that the property's title is disputed and to protect the lender's interest until the lawsuit (foreclosure) is resolved.

   For our purposes, web scraping every incoming lawsuit is the first step in our lead generation process. This Lis Pendens also includes the default date and amount owed, which are the initial building blocks to estimating equity so we can see if the property is worth pursuing. This document rarely includes the property address, but that's a simple cross-referencing task we can automate. More on that process later.

   The important thing is that data mining the Lis Pendens records before a final judgment has been issued by the court gives us a big head start over everyone else. We can now estimate with close accuracy the total payoff debt load and the home's value, thus giving us a firm estimate of how much equity is in the property. Then we screen the list for the best deals and track down the owners before every other investor jumps on the distressed homeowner.

Note: Most states only require the lawsuit notice, but a few also want a Notice of Default to be filed X days before the Lis Pendens. In that case, the default notice will serve the same research purpose for us as the Lis Pendens.

2) *Judgment.* One to six months later, the local court then decides a final judgment amount for the lender, which includes the outstanding loan balance, plus late fees, interest and attorney fees. This is the amount the lender is entitled to collect from the property's auction sale. The owner has many legal options to delay this judgment, but the longer it takes the higher the judgement amount will be and the more equity gets eaten up by the lender.

Now we're at the point when competition for the property really heats up. Instead of estimating equity, so many cash investors will wait until the final judgement is posted publicly before approaching the homeowner in a distressed sale. Hence why data mining, estimating equity and contacting the owner as early as possible are so important. If you haven't already closed a deal to take title from the homeowner by now, it's likely time to move on. The phone is going to be busy every time you call and any fliers you send out will get lost in the mountain of tacky cash-offer post cards bulging out of their mailbox.

3) *Sale.* In most judicial foreclosure states, the lender must put the property up for public auction within a certain time frame, usually around three months. Nowadays, these are mostly done online through the local county's courthouse. There are minor variations in auction methods among the 3,000+ counties nationwide, but the key aspects are universal.

The lender will make the opening bid, which may be public or hidden (a blind auction).

If the final auction sales price is higher than the lender's judgment, then any proceeds over that amount (called the surplus) are distributed to other interested parties through the priority of liens system. While there are some "super lien" exceptions from state to state, generally this means anything left over after paying off the first mortgage owner goes to each lien holder in the chronological order their lien was recorded. If there are no other liens on record, the entire surplus goes to the homeowner, or to an investor that purchased the homeowner's interest.

If you win the auction, you'll have to make an X% of your bid deposit immediately. You'll only have a small window of time, usually less than 24 hours, to finish your due diligence on the property and make final payment or forfeit your deposit.

Note: While rare, a handful of states, such as Delaware, use a so-called "strict foreclosure" process. Instead of an auction, the court sets a final redemption date a few months in the future. If the defendant (homeowner) does not settle the mortgage by then, the court awards full ownership of the home to the plaintiff (mortgage holder). Much like a repossession. At this point, the home becomes a Real Estate Owned (REO) property that will be put up on the MLS for sale at market rates.

4) *Redemption.* In most states, if the homeowner hasn't paid off or settled the debt before the auction begins, then they're out of luck. Since their interest in the home has been wiped out, if they're still living in the property, they'll be evicted by the new owner. However, a few states allow an additional redemption period after the final sale. This redemption period hold prevents the new owner from assuming full title and reselling the property for a time, sometimes as short as a few days or even as long as six months.

Opportunities and Challenges

The biggest disadvantage here is all the equity eaten up in legal fees and how difficult it is for investors to estimate before they purchase how much equity will be left over. Which isn't so bad, because turning those two challenges into competitive advantages is the point of our lead generation process. Once you've conquered those issues, you'll find three new and low-risk ways to profit from judicial foreclosures. We'll cover these strategies point by point later, but here's the overview:

1) In every state, the home owner can stop foreclosure at any time before the sale by paying off their default amount and bringing their account current, or by settling the final judgement amount if one has been issued.

   This is where angel investors like yourself come into play, as long as you reach the owner fast. You can gain title cheaply from the homeowner, then either quickly put the house up for sale and pay off the debt with the new buyer's funds, or negotiate a short payoff or cash-for-keys arrangement directly with the lender.

   Either way, you're gaining early access to a property before it gets to market, which allows you to turn most of the equity that would otherwise be wiped out at auction into cash in your pocket. For the homeowner, you're taking away the soul-crushing stress and credit destruction that comes with foreclosure away, while turning their debt into a chunk of cash in their pocket. For the lender, they're gaining a quick payoff without having to go through the expense, hassle and risk of foreclosing. A win-win-win scenario across the board.

2) Unfortunately, not everyone thinks so rationally. Some folks will always see business as a zero-sum game, filled with only winners or losers. Or maybe their hands are really tied, such as if you're dealing with a multi-million-dollar property mortgaged by a small non-bank lender. The lone claims agent, who also doubles as the CEO, keeps getting an earful from his investors threatening to jump ship and put him out of business if he settles for one cent less than the final judgement. So in this case, I'm going to do him a favor and help him show his investors how much they're losing

by being so obstinate. If nothing else, the lender's lawyer is going to love me for helping them buy a new BMW.

If for some reason the lender doesn't want to cooperate and work out a mutually beneficial arrangement, then this judicial process affords you abundant chances to fight the foreclosure. Your legal position is quite strong. You used a quitclaim deed to gain all the homeowner's interest and rights to the property, minus any explicit or implicit agreement to litigate on their behalf, of course.

This all makes you a party with indispensable interest in the property, who's not named on the original Lis Pendens. By the way, you'll be surprised how long it takes many lenders to update the lawsuit to even include you. Just one of the countless little mistakes they make that you can leverage into many more months of delay. Also, you never signed any promissory note. They don't have one scrap of paper with your signature on it. In fact, can they produce every single disclosure form and supporting document dating back to the loan's origination, including from all the mortgage servicers it has passed through? Can the plaintiff prove they have the legal right to foreclose and haven't violated any consumer protection laws in the process?

Afterall, this is a *judicial* proceeding first and foremost. They're the plaintiff claiming damages, so the burden of proof rests with them. And best of all, in a legal war of attrition, you have the cost-effectiveness edge here. The minutia of the strategy can get rather complex, but the weapons you're firing are relatively simple and cheap forms, just filed at the right time and in a particular order. Every salvo in this exchange costs you only a fraction as much as the plaintiff in attorney fees, since you're paying only for document prep and filing, while they have to spend many more hours chasing down records and responding.

With the right motion filing strategy, you can delay the sale for several years. At the moment, my longest defensive position in a judicial foreclosure is just under six years old, with no end in sight. In the meantime, you can do what I'm doing. Rent out the property at a generous profit, since your overhead is next to nothing, while putting more pressure on the lender to come to the bargaining table.

3) Well, that was fun while it lasted but all good things must come to an end. Your last motion was denied, an auction date has been set and the judge threatened you with bodily harm if you waste any more of their time with this nonsense. *C'est la vie.*

Actually, the fun is just getting started. When you do finally go to auction, remember that you've taken over the homeowner's interest. Which means you'll be entitled to any surplus at the auction. So you could potentially sit back and profit handsomely even while having your interest stripped away.

Or maybe there's still enough equity left over to make the investment worth your while. So use your position to vastly outbid everyone else and buy the property, since any amount over the judgement will be returned to you. Granted, the legal details are a bit involved and vary state to state. That's why it's crucial to check with your lawyer and make sure you're doing everything right in your local jurisdiction, but that's a snapshot of the profitable fun you can have with judicial foreclosures.

Non-Judicial or Statutory Foreclosure

This is the streamlined foreclosure approach that lets the lender bypass the courts and bring the property straight to auction. It's quite common in some of the hottest real estate markets, such as Arizona, California, Nevada, Texas and Washington. There are many procedural differences across states, but in broad strokes the process follows a simple A) notify B) advertise and C) auction flow:

1) *Notice.* After at least four months in default, the lender issues a Notice of Default to the borrower, but which is also recorded in the public records. We'll data mine these records and generate our leads from them just as if they were a Lis Pendens in a judicial proceeding. The primary difference between the two documents is that there will be more competition with non-judicial notices of default.

85

Because many of these non-judicial states do not allow deficiency judgments, or only allow them later in the foreclosure under certain conditions, this initial notice of default is enough for anyone to calculate equity. You won't have the head start over other cash investors like you would when studying the Lis Pendens for judicial foreclosures, so putting your data to use smarter and faster than everyone else is the key.

Since we're in a race to get these distressed homeowners on the line before the cash investors start a bidding war, here's where the automation, skip tracing and contact strategies we'll cover soon really pay off.

2)   *Notice of Trustee Sale.* Usually after a certain redemption period for the homeowner, typically 1-4 months, the lender is able to set a date for the auction by filing an advertisement notice. In some situations though, depending on how contracts are structured and local statutory requirements, lenders may be able to skip the public notice of default and go straight to the Trustee Sale notice. Or issue a combined notice of default and sale if the owner has been in default for an extended period.

3)   *Auction.* This part works just like public auctions in judicial proceedings, with the same priority of liens schedule and bidding process. The primary difference is that since many lenders won't have an inflated deficiency judgment, they're more likely to set their initial bid quite high.

Opportunities and Challenges

We'll still follow the same general strategies as in judicial proceedings, it's just that there's less room for error because the competition is more intense.

On the plus side, these types of foreclosed properties have much more equity in them, since we're not talking about potentially years of back interest and attorney fees tacked onto the default amount. On the other hand, everyone learns that information at the same time, so don't be surprised if the owner accepts your offer verbally, but then calls you back to shop around someone else's deal before you can send the paperwork. Still, if you follow the details in this book and online course, you'll have an edge in these negotiations. Unlike the other investors, you won't be following some seriously flawed value/equity guesses. You'll be able to draw a much finer line between equity and your maximum allowable offer and turn a major profit despite the higher acquisition costs.

You also still have legal recourse to pressure the lender into negotiating or even stopping the foreclosure, even though this is a bit more complicated. Instead of defending yourself, as with judicial foreclosures, you'll have to sue the lender and seek a temporary restraining order or even injunction to halt the foreclosure. This is totally different than judicial foreclosure delay strategies, since you're asking for an immediate decision from the court rather than trying to postpone a decision as long as possible.

Still, these non-judicial foreclosures only allow the lender to bypass the courts if they jump through several hoops. So you'll be surprised how often you can find a procedural violation that gives you a strong legal case to at least get a temporary restraining order. Once you've thrown off the lender's plans for a quick auction sell and added more red ink to their ledger, they tend to become a little more flexible when you approach them for a short payoff deal. In either case, you'll definitely need a strong foreclosure litigation attorney on your team.

Regardless of whether you're working on a judicial or non-judicial foreclosure, remember that only the loans are being foreclosed upon, and the property is just the collateral. Which means it's possible to have more than one foreclosure going on simultaneously, each at a different phase of the process. So it's important to keep up regular searches for any other Lis Pendens tied to the asset you're acquiring, even if you have already done a title search.

Flipping Or Renting Pre-Foreclosure Properties – From A-Z

Phase One: Initial Screening

So let's take a moment to put all these resources and decisions into a simple workflow process. There might be some minor variations in your state or county when executing each step, but here's how everything comes together from A-Z.

Again, the goal is to find lender pre-foreclosures with built-in equity, generate detailed leads and contact them with as little human intervention on your part as possible. This should be your general template for finding and filtering all potential deals, but we'll cover the specific extra steps for auction preparation and HOA foreclosures in the next chapter.

You're actually running four different scraper programs on three different websites, at a minimum. Each of which runs searches for specific bits of data (pull requests) and fills in part of the puzzle. Most of the time, all of this data can be extracted by your automated scraper scripts, but depending on how your county structures their website, some human searching might be necessary. In this case, you can hire a cheap virtual assistant, such as from Upwork to conduct the search manually and fill in the missing data fields.

Note: to keep your costs down, these are the bare minimum pieces of information you need to pull automatically. There are many other data points that are useful to estimating equity, 93 according to my current Excel sheet, but we don't need to pull them all at this stage. Most of them we can fill in later at the due diligence phase, when we've filtered out the riff-raff, made a hard offer that's been accepted and we're looking for final confirmation that we should pull the trigger on the deal.

Remember, here we're just screening for opportunities. Finding homeowners that aren't underwater and have sizeable equity in their home. Later in the process we'll go over step by step how you dive deeper and manually evaluate these potential deals.

Step 1: Find recent Lis Pendens

The first objective is to scrape all recent Lis Pendens recorded on your local Public Records or Clerk of Courts website and send the details to your master data sheet. If your state allows non-judicial judgments, then you should also scrape for Notice of Defaults, which for our research goals serve the same purpose as a Lis Pendens.

The vast majority of counties in the US keep these records in a simple publicly searchable website that's open to everyone, but a few counties in really hot housing markets might restrict access for these particular notices to "real estate professionals." In which case, just consult with your lawyer for a subscription to a good local title search service and you're good to go. It's an annoying but small cost of doing business, and one that's well worth the trouble.

The key outputs you want to pull from each lawsuit are:

- Document ID – The notice ID # of the Lis Pendens itself. Since many of these documents have all the important details included as hard to scrape scanned PDF attachments, we'll need to send the doc number to our virtual assistants for them to manually look up information.

- Plaintiff Name – Knowing who is foreclosing, such as a national bank, local bank, non-bank online lender, another investor or individual will help you estimate final judgment and the chances of a short sale.

- Defendant 1 Name – While this is pulled from the website once, make sure the names are populated into your data base with the first and last names in separate cells so there aren't mistakes in step 2.

- Defendant 2 Name – If applicable, such as with a cosigner or married couple. Later we might filter these multi party properties out of our list to reduce risk, but right now we're looking for raw data.

- Record Date – When Lis Pendens was recorded. Make sure you copy the timestamp as well as date. In some cases, you might have multiple foreclosures striking on the same day.

- Case # – To track all activity on the foreclosure.

- Default Date – The date when the account first went into default. The older the default, the higher fees you should estimate for the final judgment.

- Default Amount – Here is the remaining 1st mortgage debt on the loan. Later, we'll add other liens, unpaid taxes and an estimated final judgment assessment to calculate the available equity.

Step 2: Find the property address

Since the Lis Pendens will usually not include the property address, your next script searches the county's property appraiser's site, using the defendant's name as in input for the "search parcel by owner name" or equivalent search criteria. This is the most likely step where you might run into search areas that leave some fields blank. For example, the property appraiser's site might record the owner's full middle name and the lawsuit might give just their middle initial. Again, a cheap virtual assistant can fill in the gaps fast for you.

Depending on how your local county site is structured, you'll likely run two searches here. The first is to find the **Parcel Number**, sometimes called the folio number.

With the parcel number in hand, you can then run another script on the same site that searches that parcel number for the following details:

- Property Address – Note: the original pull request goes into one cell for easy reference, but then the data should be separated into different cells by street #/name, city, state & zip for step 3.

- Mailing Address

In addition, here are some of the scores of optional data points that will help you spot outliers or special conditions. You can pull this now or wait until after you've weeded down the list:

- Date Bought – The last sale of the home

- Price of Last Sale

- Number of Units or Beds/Baths

- Property type and/or neighborhood, such as condos, SFH, etc… if you're focusing on a particular niche.

Step 3: Pull the Zillow estimated price for that address

This is the easiest part, since Zillow's API allows up to 1,000 free calls a day. Naturally, the Zestimate is far from perfect. Especially for properties outside of a subdivision or apartment/condo development, but it's fine for our purposes at the moment of just narrowing down are list of leads to the hottest potential deals.

Once you have the Zestimate downloaded, then you can populate the final cell in that property's row with the Zillow price minus the default amount. Label this "estimated equity." Right now we're using this just to weed out underwater homes (anything with a negative value).

Step 3.1: Estimated Equity

This Estimated Equity field is the most important column in your entire spreadsheet because this value decides what you're going to invest in and how much you're willing to spend. So calculating equity after the initial screening is not something you want to delegate to an assistant. Once you're ready to start contacting homeowners and preparing offers, you need to be hands-on and double check everything. Remember, you can earn easy passive income or you can get rich, but not both.

Most important of all, your equity estimate is a running tally that's never truly "finished," since a hundred different details could pop up to improve or hurt that number. Yes, with this data-driven approach we are only working with the most lucrative investments that have a significant equity cushion built into the equation, but we don't want to just minimize risk—we also want to maximize reward. So if you stay on top of your equity at every step of the process, you'll be able to rein in your expenses, know when you should hold out for a better offer or settle for what you have, and in the worst-case scenarios, pull out of a contract well before the expenses reach critical mass.

91

You'll need to refine this estimate for each property you're interested in manually every time a new bit of data comes along. At a minimum though, you'll want to update the Estimated Equity by subtracting any new costs for you or new property debt or changes to the expected sales price at the following stages:

- After pulling the Zestimate and subtracting from the default amount (Step 3 here).

- After conducting your manual research on the best potential deals (as outlined in Phase 2 ahead).

- After finding and talking with the homeowner to discover their goals and pain points, but before you make a firm offer (as outlined in Phase 4 ahead).

- Right after negotiations are complete and your offer is accepted. Deduct the new title transfer costs from the estimated equity.

- After your title search and walk-through with your contractors to determine the state of the property and rehab costs, but in the due diligence phase before you close. This is really the last chance for any big surprises to hit you, such as structural issues with the property or an undetected second mortgage. If any of these issues break your minimum equity threshold, then you'll still have a chance to back out of the deal at the last minute if you've structured the contracts as recommended in Phase 4.

- Every month you're holding the property until it's sold. Double check your expected sales price and deduct your monthly holding costs to keep the equity estimate up to date. If you're renting the property out and generating a profit every month,

- When negotiating with buyers, keep updating until the deal closes. Even if they offer the asking price, there are all sorts of little issues that can change the equity equation. Such as needing to offer credits or cash for closing costs to keep a troubled buyer from backing out at the last second.

Step 4: Filter by equity and your niche

Here, you simply sort the data with the Estimated Equity going from highest to lowest. Obviously, you can ignore anything with negative equity. If the list is particularly long, and it likely will be in any sizeable metropolitan area, you can further sort this list by your preferred niche. If you're still unsure what to focus on, I'd recommend sorting by the highest equity homes in cities/neighborhoods that you know are popular or the newest homes first or those with the most recent default date (will likely have the least competition).

I also like to remove any entries where the owner is an estate or LLC. For obvious reasons, I prefer to deal with regular homeowners rather than savvy investors or lawyers.

Phase Two: Manual Research

Now for the fun part. We're going to go through those hot picks and make sure they tick every block on our investment checklist. This may seem daunting at first, but this part is the secret sauce that gives you a huge leg up on the competition and saves you a fortune by ensuring there aren't any big surprises in the future.

Step 1: Update the amount owed

This alone is a multi-step process, but it's essentially an unofficial title search. We want to add up all the known debt and estimate what the foreclosure's final judgement amount will be to make sure there's enough meat in the meal. While it's difficult to get the debt load absolutely right, I'm usually within 5% of the final payoff amount just by searching the public records, property appraiser's and tax collector's websites for the following:

- Add 1.5 percentage points to every month the 1st lender's debt has been in default and multiply that by the default amount to estimate the final judgement. This is a conservative way to calculate what we expect the lender demands to cover their back interest, late fees and legal costs, as well as our legal and administration costs while negotiating with them. For example, if the home went into default six months ago with an outstanding balance of $200k, I would estimate the lender wants $218k to pay off the mortgage.

  If this feels too pessimistic, remember the old saying: "nothing gets eaten as hot as it gets cooked." In practice, you can almost always work out a final settlement out of court for significantly less, thereby unlocking more equity. However, in this pre-purchase stage, it's all about managing risk by budgeting for worst-case scenarios. This seemingly small point gives us a major head start on most investors, since we can estimate equity long before them.

- Any 2nd mortgages, HELOC loans, etc… even if they aren't yet in default.

- Any other liens, such as from a home owner's association or code violations. We'll double check right before closing to make sure no new liens have been filed.

- Any outstanding property taxes. Note: if the current year's status is not yet available, assume it's unpaid.

Step 2: Update the property value

Here we're going to use the property appraiser's recent nearby sales data as an unofficial Comparative Market Analysis (CMA). We'll do a more accurate CMA in the final phase, after we've made contact with the owner and confirmed they're interested in selling at a reasonable price. At this point, we're just looking to make sure we have enough equity in the deal to proceed. Quite a few of your hot picks will likely be weeded out in this phase because the margins are too tight, so we don't want to waste too much time here.

You can ignore the home's "assessed value" or "just market value" and look at recent "comp" sales. Like with a comprehensive CMA, we're looking for at least three recent comparable sales to get a rough idea what price we can realistically sell this home. You could also do this on Zillow, but the appraiser's office usually makes it easier to see the more accurate final recorded sale price, less any credits or other considerations. At a minimum, you want to screen these comps for the following, in descending order of importance:

- Look only at normal "qualified" sales. Discard anything listed as a distressed, disqualified for assessment or short sale.

- Consider sales closer to the target home as the "best" comps. Generally, even a home that sold on the same block that's a couple years older and 5% or so smaller still gives you a closer estimate than one that's a perfect age and size match but a mile away.

- Matching comps by the same number of units/beds/baths is more valuable than square footage, assuming the size difference isn't more than +/- 10%.

If your comps aren't close matches, then take the average as your expected value. If they are quite similar, then take the lowest value as your estimate. Better to err on the side of caution at this stage.

Note: Always double check the legal description between the Lis Pendens or Notice of Default matches exactly what's shown on the property appraiser's site. You'll be surprised how often even a major lender tries to foreclose on the wrong house. Or they might have the right house but left in a little typo that requires an updated Lis Pendens. A useful bit of info to have on hand in case you need to delay the foreclosure later.

So when you add all this up, you'll have a far better estimate of the equity involved and the price you should offer, and have this on hand well before any other investor makes an offer. Most flippers prefer to wait until the final judgment comes in before running these numbers, so you're ahead of the curve. You can now apply your 70/30 rule or other measure to figure out your maximum allowed offer, with exponentially more confidence and less risk.

Of course, all this advanced data isn't going to do much good if you can't contact the owner faster, smarter and more tactfully than any other investor.

Phase Three: Lead Generation

Step 1: Skip Tracing

We need more contact info than just the mailing address. Here's the part where many investors who are otherwise incredibly thorough throw away their advantage. The mailing address is public info, so everyone is sending out snail mail flyers. Sure, maybe yours comes first, but it's still merely one more letter in a stack of all-cash offers, assuming they even bother opening it after wading through their bills and other junk mail.

If you want an edge that guarantees you'll stand out from the pack, close deals faster and at a lower cost, then you have to go the extra mile. You're going to do what most investors don't bother with. You're going to hire a skip-tracing service to get the phone numbers of these prospects before anyone else.

Now, I realize that "skip tracing" is a loaded term with negative connotations that often makes new entrepreneurs squeamish, but this isn't an optional step. We're not debt collectors nor bounty hunters. We're not doing anything illegal or even in a legal grey area. The only information we're collecting are publicly listed current phone numbers associated with a particular address. Our research is far less invasive than looking at someone's Facebook page, for example, since we're only after a single data point—their phone number. This is the same lead generation process that millions of businesses in other industries use on a daily basis, yet for some reason it hasn't caught on so well in the real estate world.

Which is great, because it means even more opportunities for you. Even if you happen to be competing with some top-tier investors in your local market, then skip tracing is even more critical since speed and tact will decide the winner.

I use LexisNexus for this service, but there are many firms out there that can deliver similar results. Since the task is relatively simple, you're looking for a company that can produce reports within 24 hours for only a few dollars per person of interest (POI). Regardless of what company you plan to engage, stress four things when you contact them to get the best quote:

- You have each POI's full legal name and recent address.

- You only need phone numbers associated with that name and address. No other information is required.

- You're a high-volume customer, with dozens to hundreds of requests every month.

- You're looking for a recurring subscription-based payment plan to keep costs down, rather than a pay as you go plan.

Step 2: Customer resource management (CRM) and virtual assistant integration

At this point you have several Excel sheets full of data. We need to import everything we've gathered so far, including the incoming phone numbers, into your preferred CRM program. Besides keeping things organized, this will also let us automate, delegate and track the initial customer contacts. Which frees up more time for you to research properties and find new potential deals.

There are a ton of off-the-shelf CRM programs you could use for this step. I built my own customized program, which in my online course I show even non-coders how to duplicate, but that's optional. If you're going with a 3rd party solution, the most important feature is to make sure it includes built-in Voice Over Internet (VOIP) calling.

Your CRM module is going to be your phone bank and sole depository for all customer information. If any new details about the customer or the property come to light later, make sure you update them here instead of just keeping notes somewhere else. You have a huge data advantage at the moment; a list of hot leads of pre-vetted and motivated sellers with sizeable equity in their homes that even most local agents don't know about. So organization is key to putting this data to the best use.

One of the most common mistakes at this point is conducting follow up calls or emails with leads outside the program. Every phone call, text and email from initial contact to final closing needs to go through this CRM communications portal. Even the details of any offline, face to face chats should be noted and tracked in your CRM. You're dealing with a ton of leads, each with a sizeable amount of data that needs to be tracked, and perhaps even multiple points of contact.

On the same token, it's important that you have a live human available to respond to leads 24/7. It's such a shame at this point to miss a phone call or take too long to answer a question. We want to generate leads for ourselves, not for everyone else. What if your initial SMS message peeked their interest, but they can't get a hold of you immediately? So they go online and search Google for "sale my home as is for fast cash" and whistle at all the results. You can bet one of those services will respond immediately, without even dropping you a thank-you note for generating free business for them.

You must have additional virtual assistants ready with scripts to respond after work hours or during "overflow" periods when you and your primary assistants are busy on other calls. Whether you hire dedicated agents through Upwork or engage a 3rd party firm with their own call center, you need these people in place ahead of time and armed with answers to common questions.

One final note: your skip tracing will often return multiple phone numbers and names associated with an address. Usually family members that have at one point or another used this property address on a public database. So it's important to organize your leads by the property address, with each number or mailing address grouped under that lead as a point of contact.

Sample initial contact letter

I know I bashed physical mailings earlier, but they are a useful outreach tool in some situations. Especially if you're having trouble getting a call back from your text messages.

Dear <owner_first_name> <owner_last_name>,

My name is ___. I work for a real estate company that represents a network of investors across the state. I'm contacting you today because one of my clients has evaluated your home's condition and asked me to forward an "as is" cash offer for your property at <Owner_street_address>.

It appears as though <plaintiff_name> has begun foreclosure proceedings against your home in __ county's courthouse. I understand how unfair and frustrating this situation must be for you, which is why my client is willing to help by purchasing your property 100% as-is with a cash payment. They will immediately take over the mortgage loan and all other liens or taxes owed on the property.

If you have no interest in moving away and you're only being forced to abandon your home because of the foreclosure and impending eviction, we have several options to help you stay there debt-free. In some cases, we can even purchase the property and lease it back to you at a reasonable rental rate. In all cases though, we will take over the property's debt, freeing you completely from the financial burden you currently face, as well as put immediate cash in your pocket in exchange for assuming the property's ownership.

Please note that my client is only able to work out a deal before the foreclosure process is complete. At that point, the bank will take control and put the home up for sale at auction. Since you have only a short window of time to work out a solution to this problem, it's important that you contact me by phone at ___ or email at ___ as soon as possible. Even if you've found a good lawyer to fight the bank, it doesn't hurt to find out what your back up options are. So please feel free to send me any questions you have, big or small.

Phase Four: Making Contact and Sending Offers

I know we've covered a lot of ground and it seems like we have so much little trivia to keep track of, but once you've gone through this process a few times it will become an easy routine. You'll never go back to expensive direct mailing campaigns or buying stale leads through 3ʳᵈ party firms. Remember, the real work is just setting up the software, scripts, assistant workflow and general infrastructure in the first place. Once your system is in place, all of this can run automatically, with your assistant filling in any missing details.

Your job is just sifting through the best options and double-checking equity/value. Let others handle the dirty mining work while you spend your time as a jeweler, studying and appraising these diamonds in the ruff for value.

Now take a step back and look at everything you've done in perspective. It might seem like just a bunch of admin work and number crunching, but you've accomplished something that most real estate investors and even professional agents would envy. Take a second to savor the fruits of your labors. In a couple of hours, you've put together a reliable, ultra-detailed list of scores of hot pre-foreclosure leads that few, if any, other investors know about... and you're sending the homeowners messages to their cell phone the *same day* the Lis Pendens is posted.

The competitive advantage you've just created out of thin air can't be exaggerated. For example, many of my clients first discovered they were even in foreclosure from me, sometimes days before the court server could notify them of the suit. And best of all, well before any other distressed property investor could contact them and bid up the price.

Converting Leads to Clients: Where The Rubber Meets The Road

With everything set up, we can now start contacting these homeowners and opening up negotiations. One of the great things here is that we can send personalized batch texts and even physical letters with little human effort. Just create templates in your CRM and let the system input the custom information for each contact. Then you can contact hundreds of leads with the push of a button. Besides saving you and your assistants a vast amount of time, this helps make sure you can reach out to these leads minutes after receiving their information.

With that said, how you initially approach prospects, the general methods, context and exact wording, needs to be as carefully considered as everything else you do. For some reason, I see so many otherwise clever investors sending out short and informal texts or general, non-customized flyers. I wonder why they even went to the trouble of researching leads in the first place if they're going to put so little effort into converting these prospects.

Step 1: Test your points of contact to find the primary decision maker

Quite often, your skip tracing will return multiple phone numbers and it's not always clear which one leads to someone qualified to sell the house. There are likely phone numbers for family members, ex's, business associates or even neighbors mixed into the list. So if there's any ambiguity about who you're contacting, the first step is to batch text every number to find the primary decision maker.

This obviously requires a bit of finesse, since even if the homeowner is ready to sale, they could rightfully be annoyed if you're spreading details of their financial situation to 3rd parties.

So this initial contact message needs to be neutral, with little information, yet still interesting enough to make sure they respond. All while avoiding any signs of "spam." Which is easier than it sounds, since we've collected so much information on the lead already.

Note: there are some federal regulations governing these types of "cold calls," which all boil down to common sense and human decency. Such as only contact between the hours of 8 am and 9 pm, do not misrepresent your service (i.e. no bait-and-switch) and respect the prospect's right to be removed from your contact list if they ask. Just like with every strategy outlined in this book, it's important to check that your local and state laws don't have any additional restrictions.

Sample Finding the Homeowner SMS:

"Hello, I'm trying to reach <defendant_1_First_name/Last_name> or <defendant_2_First_name/Last_name> on behalf of my client, who is interested in purchasing their property as soon as possible. We only have a short window of time before he invests elsewhere and I'm not sure if I have the right phone number. Thank you for your time and assistance. – [Your full name and company name]"

There are many ways you can word this, but the key themes you should hit are:

1. Lead with who you're trying to contact, rather than who you are, which usually disarms the knee-jerk "spam" response most people have to unsolicited messages.

2. Follow up with a short but interesting and time sensitive description of your offer. It's important to pass along urgency without being pushy. Avoid spam-like wording such as "as is condition" or "all cash offer." Always aim for emotionless terms, such as using "property" instead of "home."

3. Do not ask any "yes/no" questions. If there's no immediate action option for them to take in response, they'll have to think about what to do instead of reflexively saying no and deleting the text. Most people will reread the message to make sure they understand your meaning, giving a better chance that your message will sink in. Simple engagement is the goal at this point and this all increases the likelihood they'll respond with follow up questions.

4. To reiterate: make no explicit or even implicit mention of "debt" or "foreclosure" or any other negative point until you are 100% positive you're speaking to the homeowner and doing so in private. This means even identifying yourself as a "foreclosure expert." These are sensitive subjects and the people you're contacting are not usually in the best mood. It doesn't matter how great your offer is if you insult them by airing their dirty laundry in front of others.

Step 2: Learn the owner's endgame

By this point, you should have found the primary homeowner and established rudimentary contact. This might be as simple as a, "Yeah, that's me" response, but at least you now have your foot in the door. Whether this is a judicial or statutory foreclosure, you are light years ahead of everyone relying on a snail mail outreach campaign, and you did so at a fraction of the cost.

Now, we know what the homeowner's general situation is and how much we can afford to spend on purchasing the house, but that's still not enough to make a definitive offer. Before we can quote a figure, we need to chat on the phone with the owner and find out a few key pieces of information. The goal right now isn't to ask them whether or not they're willing to transfer the title. If they're motivated to sell ASAP, they'll let you know immediately. More often than not, they're not ready to sell for some reason, or else they would have sold the home long before the bank came calling. We need to figure out what obstacle is in the way and how can we help them.

And I can't stress that enough. You're not some hyena roving the plains for fresh corpses to pick over; you're an angel investor coming to save lost and injured souls. Maybe you think this sounds cheesy or naïve, but it works. If you aren't legitimately willing to help with their unique circumstances, even if that means parting with a little more money than you originally estimated, then you'll miss out on the nuance of what they're saying and all the opportunities that entails. Not to mention they'll notice your unsympathetic, "circling shark" demeanor and will have their guard up. The more empathetic you are, the more likely you are to establish real rapport and trust. You don't have to be their best friend or even like them, but if you are able to truly put yourself in your prospect's shoes and think about what you'd like to hear if you and your family were in their situation, then you will excel at these discussions. That's the simple secret of great salesmanship in any industry right there.

So our questions during that initial call should center on learning their specific needs and testing solutions. Once you find out their game plan, you can make them an offer that fixes their problem rather than just negotiating up until your maximum allowed bid. That might sound like a minor distinction, but this nuance is crucial to unlocking even more equity in the deal.

Step 3: Most common responses from distressed homeowners and simple solutions

Response 1: Owner understands how much equity they have in the home and refuses to sell at a steep discount.

Solution: Find out their end game. Are they hoping on negotiating some settlement with the bank or a traditional home sale? Gently point out how that ship has already sailed. Stress how their equity is evaporating fast with all the extra interest and attorney fees, plus they'll need extra cash to get the home ready for sale, all while they're racing against the foreclosure clock. Add in agent fees and no time to hold out for a good offer and they'll be lucky to have any equity left over.

And don't just talk in the abstract. Show them the numbers you ran on their home. Share your information on the estimated final judgment debt and realistic fast home sale price (not just current value). In most cases, a quick cash sell to you would truly leave them with far more money in their pockets, without all the risk or stress. The fastest way to convince them is to show them your data.

Worst case scenario, you wind up losing all your bargaining room and pay top-dollar for the property. Doesn't matter, since you still built in at least a 25% equity cushion in the deal or you wouldn't have called them. The key thing is you're still converting this hot lead and closing the deal fast, before anyone else. Smaller profit, but safe and rapid deals are a great way to build a sustainable real estate empire.

Response 2: Owner flat out says they have no interest in moving, no matter what price you offer. Seller refuses to leave for sentimental or other life reasons and plans on "getting a lawyer to fight those SOB's."

Solution: No problem. This might seem like a deal breaker at first, because all they're doing is delaying the inevitable foreclosure and chewing up equity in the meantime. And no, it's not the ideal flipping opportunity, but there's still some serious money to be made for all parties in this situation. It's also the type of scenario where we can really shine as angel investors by purchasing the deed and offering to lease the home back at current market rates.

Instead of trying to change their mind, I'll point out how that's a great idea. Where other investors are backing out at this point or mentioning all the flaws with their plan, I'm going to work with the owner and help them make their dream come true. I'll offer some tips on the foreclosure delay approach and explain how, if they get a good attorney that's really working in their interest, they could delay the foreclosure for years.

Even better, after we've established a little rapport and they have a general understanding of everything that's involved, I'll offer a lease-back option. I'll assume title and fight the bank on their behalf. I'll pay all the attorney fees and lease the place back to them with a much lower rent than their current mortgage.

Instead of facing years of mounting legal bills, stress and uncertainty, which will only culminate in a credit-destroying foreclosure and eventual eviction, I can make all those problems go away right now. They don't have to move and disrupt their life. I can even sweeten the pot by tossing in an immediate cash bonus. Turning their crippling debt into a quick nest egg.

Now, I know what you're thinking at this point. "Why would I want a tenant with such a poor payment history?" And it's true. The unfortunate reality is that most homeowners who are unable or unwilling to pay their mortgage are not going to pay their rent, even if the price goes down significantly.

If they do keep paying on time and in full, great. That rent is mostly profit for you, since your holding costs are next to nothing. You'll likely recover your paltry initial investment in just a few months too. And you still have plenty of options for a big "pay day" down the road, since you can negotiate a short payoff with the bank, wholesale to another rental-focused investor or even buy back the property at a discount during the foreclosure auction.

However, far too often, the owner winds up defaulting within just two or three months of starting the new lease. You've done what you could to help, but it's time to cancel the lease and activate your writ of possession. Depending on how stringent the eviction laws in your state are, you should have the home clear and ready to sell on the market within a few months. In my online course, I cover the legal minutia of how to safely structure these lease back deals and head off problems in advance.

Response 3: Homeowner wants to sell but lacks the financial means to relocate.

Solution: This is one of those ideal scenarios that lets you negotiate in relation to what the owner needs, rather than just against your best offer. In this situation, usually the owner has more pressing debt than the mortgage, so they're willing to "leave some money on the table" if it means getting quick cash.

So let's say your research gives you a top-line offer on a property at $30k. You plan on opening with $15k and then negotiate from there. However, once you start talking to the prospect and get a sense of their life situation, you realize they're really motivated to sell. For example, when they keep asking about how fast this process takes. So instead of a traditional negotiation, you dig deeper and ask them exactly what obstacles are in the way of them moving out. Then you tally those expenses up with the client.

They'll need a security deposit for their new place, plus first and last months' rent. We should also get a moving company to speed things up. And what about their car payments? Are they behind? In most places in America, having your auto repossessed is even worse than foreclosure. How are they going to get to work?

So together you've added up an easy $10k in expenses. Then you mention you can handle that. Even top it off with another $5k in walking around money so the owner can celebrate and treat their family to a little vacation. And naturally, you'll cover all closing costs.

Now your "low ball" offer seems incredibly generous. Too good to pass up. After all, this is still a win-win situation for everyone. Maybe they could hold out for a better deal, but no one understands their problems better than you. And you're offering to make all their troubles go away, to change their life, *today*. You'll have the paperwork finished and the cash in their pocket in just 48 hours. That's the type of pitch that moves them into fast action. Even if a new investor comes along and offers them $20k, it's hard for most people to back away from an immediate payoff for the promise of a slightly higher one in the future.

Response 4: Owner tries to start a bidding war. Even though you've moved faster than most investors and agents, the owner has been pro-actively reaching out to various distressed property buyers and just wants to know your top-line offer. Any number you quote, they call back soon with a real or imagined offer from someone else that's always just a little higher than yours.

Solution: Boy, oh boy, I've been caught in the crossfire of countless bidding wars. Especially when a homeowner is actively seeking out offers and everyone swarms on this new "hot" lead. In this environment, it's so easy for otherwise cool and calm professionals to get sucked into the game and make emotionally charged mistakes. So when you hear the first shots fired, you need to stay rock-solid neutral. You're Switzerland, quietly getting rich while everyone else is duking it out and losing money, even when they win a war.

Once you realize you're dealing with a serious, well-informed customer, then give your best offer and stick to it, no matter what.

Once the homeowner notices you standing firm on your price, they'll try all sorts of things to tempt you. A savvy negotiator will attempt to push your buttons and make you second-guess yourself. "You know, how confident are you in your estimate of my home's value? Isn't that a conservative guess anyway? If you could just budge a *little* on your top offer, we could make this deal happen right now and you'll still make plenty of money."

That might sound reasonable, but a little is never enough. If you up your price a half-percentage point, they'll ask for a full point tomorrow. And another, and yet another. Soon, you're way past your tolerance level, but you're also so close to sealing the deal. You've invested so much time already, and just maybe you were being too pessimistic in your valuation…

No. Just. Don't.

Don't rationalize anything. Don't second-guess yourself. When I hear the drums of a bidding war brewing or any other wild stories from a homeowner, that's when my empathy fades. All that goes through my head is "Yadda yadda." Once I know I'm dealing with a savvy lead who has time for games, it's time to show them that I don't have any free play time. My standard response is:

"I understand you, but please realize my client is an active buyer with multiple investment projects in the works. I've closed many purchases with them and I can assure you they will not deviate from the budget under any circumstances. So what I'm offering you is the best price we can manage. I can lock the rate in place for 48 hours, but after that we'll have to lower the price, since the available equity in your property is shrinking fast as foreclosure approaches. If you're interested, I can prepare all the terms and forms for you to review and email that to you by the morning."

If the deal is really attractive, I'll follow up a few days later to sniff the air and see if anything's changed, but that's it. It's important to stand by everything you say. You make the best good faith offer you can tolerate and don't bother with any games. Ignore the bluffs and just lay your cards on the table. Otherwise, you're no longer an angel investor and you become just another run of the mill sales person.

Response 5: A married couple hold joint title. One wants to take your offer, but the other doesn't. Perhaps even made more complicated if the relationship is on the rocks and one spouse has moved out.

Solutions: Ideally, we would have avoided this issue in the filtering leads phase by focusing on Lis Pendens with only a single defendant. Generally, you want to deal with as few interested parties as possible, but sometimes you'll see a home with so much equity baked in that you're willing to take on these additional complications.

Yes, at the end of the day the couple is just going to have to work out the decision on their own, but there are a few things we can do to help. If it's just a typical domestic squabble, we learn the holdout's end game. Find out what he or she wants most of all and how can we make that happen, just like with the previous responses. Needless to say, it's important to stay aloof, focusing on solutions and not give them the impression you're agreeing or disagreeing with their partner.

If the couple is in the process of divorcing, then it should be even easier to convince them to sell fast. Ask to speak with their lawyers. I know that sounds weird, but I love dealing with lawyers. Maybe I lose a little profit on the margins, but I know that things will go much smoother and faster. Plus, I have a new partner in the deal that will pressure their client to accept my "generous" offer. You always need to focus on the big picture to survive and thrive in the long run.

Response 6: Owner has long since moved away and stopped paying the mortgage, while renting the home out. Perhaps even on a long-term lease. The unfortunate renter has no idea the property is facing foreclosure.

Solution: This is definitely a mixed-blessing situation. On the down side, you're buying the lease and its associated responsibilities (i.e. baggage) as well as the deed. And unlike when you're leasing back a property to the original owner, the current tenant has no particular motivation to keep the home well maintained. They're not getting any extra money out of the deal. On the plus side, the absentee owner is usually far less attached to the property and more amenable to a discounted sell. In addition, the tenant has probably been vetted and is far less likely to default.

Still, as long as you respect the terms of the lease and you have a strong foreclosure defense strategy, then you can treat this just like an HOA foreclosure. Explain the situation to your new tenant. They might not be sympathetic, but you have nothing to lose by treating them with respect. Make sure you get them on a month-to-month lease

110

as soon as you can. Adding a little extra to the security deposit, paid out of your own pocket, can always go a long to ensuring a smooth transition for the tenant. Again, don't lose sight of the big picture over a grand or two of petty cash.

Step 4: Find out what you're missing

Once your lead is warmed up, they'll probably start pressuring you to make a firm offer. Before you do so, you want to get a little information from them. If you have the time and/or the deal seems particularly lucrative, then schedule a walk-through with you, your home inspector or contractor lead.

At a minimum, you want to pump the owner for information on any other hidden costs. Make sure to stress that these aren't a "big deal" but that you're just "checking off the tick boxes on the form."

You want to know about the following, but the trick is not to ask direct, yes/no questions. Instead, stick to open ended questions that require them to take a moment and think about their response. Regardless of what they say, you can obviously read volumes from their pauses or other signs of hesitancy.

Potential building code violations. This is hands-down the biggest surprise you'll find with a property. Most of the time, the owner simply did some relatively minor improvement work on their home and never bothered getting a permit. Neither the owner nor the county even knows there's a code violation yet, but you can bet it'll come out later. Usually at the worst possible time when you're trying to resell the property, already lined up a buyer and their home inspector finds unpermitted renovations that spook the buyer's loan provider. Then you have to make hasty and expensive repairs in a hurry, since these fines for unlicensed renovations are assessed daily and add up fast.

On the plus side, discovering these problems during this initial contact call is fairly simple. At this point, you've established a bit of rapport and definitely have the owner's interest, so they're usually quite happy to brag about any improvements they've made to the property. You just need to give them a little push.

So prompt the owner to confirm the information you're seeing online, including photo-based sites like Google Street View, in a way that gets them to play up their strengths. Some of the most common non-permitted renovations are visible from the curb, such as an extra patio, attached structure, or converted garage that's not listed on the property appraiser's floor plan.

In these cases, you can simply look up the permit history on the house and see if they have one and budget accordingly.

If nothing is obviously out of place from the cursory search, then you should still go fishing. Lead with: "Great, thanks. Now before I can offer our best price, I just want to double check our records here. How many bedrooms do you have now? Can you tell me more about what condition the bathrooms are in?"

As they get bored with answering simple questions and you're just "humming" along being non-committal, they'll usually inadvertently let slip more details about improvements they've done. Then you can just ask when the addition was made and how much it cost, making it easy to look up if they have permit and if not, how much it will cost to get one. If you keep things casual, the owner won't even know that you're pumping them for information.

Unpaid Home Owner's Association Dues

While many HOA's are quick to levy obscene fines and take legal action, that doesn't always mean they've filed an official lien. That could always come out at the last possible time, usually after the HOA sees the home has changed hands and the property is getting ready for sale.

Now, it's safe to assume the owner is not paying the HOA if they aren't paying the mortgage lender, but the question is how much is owed. If you just ask, there's a good chance the owner will downplay the damage for fear of scuttling the deal.

So instead, the best way to get accurate information is to lead with sympathetic complaining about the HOA and get the owner on your side: "You know, we could close this deal much faster if I can just cut the HOA a check for back dues and fees on your behalf. So how much is the suburban mafia shaking you down for? Can you take a picture of their latest threatening letter and email that to me? I can't wait to sic my lawyer on them."

Phase Five: Pre-Closing Due Diligence

Step 1: Research the HOA's Rules and Restrictions

In many states, the by-laws of local home owners' associations supersede state law. This weird quirk of local law has a big impact on your business. So it's crucial to contact the local HOA chief directly before you close on a deal and get written confirmation (via email is enough) that everything you want to do is allowed in their bylaws. And naturally, you want confirmation from the *hefe*, the head honcho, and not some low-level rep.

For example, if you're renting the property, make sure they allow a non-owner tenant to occupy the owner. If they don't, have them specify exactly how much equity a tenant needs to rent the place. Usually you can work around this issue by offering your renter a 1% stake in the property.

If you're planning on a short-term flip, then tell them that and make sure there aren't any time or occupancy restrictions with reselling a house in a short time frame.

Sure, you can often look this information up from their website, but that's not enough. We're dealing with an extralegal jurisdiction here that is above the law and can change their own rules at any time. So if there are any issues in the future, you want to be able to show written proof that you were "grandfathered into" the old rules.

Step 2: Research the neighborhood as thoroughly as you do the home.

You know the location, location, location mantra, but what does that mean in practice for home flippers? It all boils down to one thing: how fast you can sell a property in that neighborhood. Location is quite similar for rental investors: how fast can you get a quality tenant in there who's paying better than average rent?

Landing a great deal on a home isn't exactly a win if it takes you a year or more to offload your investment or the area has poor appeal and it takes months to find a decent renter. Even if your holding costs are minimal, the opportunity costs are through the roof. How many other, even better investments are you missing out on while your capital is tied up here?

This goes double if you're focused on reselling. You should be striving to flip each home in your portfolio every four months... so a year delay means two extra deals you missed out on. Personally, it takes me 3-5 months from initial purchase offer to closing, which is an easy rate to maintain as long as you're sticking to properties in your niche, which includes an in-depth understanding of the neighborhoods you're operating in.

Ideally you would have a good understanding of the neighborhood's quality, appeal and how fast similar types of properties are selling before approaching the homeowner or placing a bid at auction. Still, when big equity opportunities present themselves, we need to be ready to spring into action even if you know nothing about the property's surroundings.

On the plus side, the key metrics you should look for in either an urban area or subdivision are rather simple to evaluate. This can all be done with a few minutes of internet research or a quick call to a listing agent that works in the area.

1) In the last year, how long on average do homes sit on the market in this neighborhood? Anything more than 180 days should be a red flag that this is not a "hot" local market. Doesn't mean you should necessarily abandon the deal, but that you should adjust your estimated equity by factoring in a whole year's worth of holding costs.

2) How intense is the competition nearby? This is where the MLS comes in handy. By nearby, I generally look at all similar units for sale within a mile radius, or in a particular subdivision or city quarter. We'll go into this in more detail in a bit, but realize that the more comparable homes for sale nearby, the deeper you'll need to discount the listing price.

3) If selling family unit housing, what is the local school district rating? The higher the school rating, the more motivated and qualified buyers you're likely to attract, which gives you more confidence that

this home is a safe bet. If the school rating is below average, you're far less likely to attract motivated buyers ready to close fast. Note: just like with everything, double check the accuracy of the listing's assigned school district. It's common to find sellers accidentally or intentionally misreporting which school district a property falls under, so check the local school's website to verify the zoning.

4) What is the home's value relative to the neighborhood's average value? Regardless of how accurate your CMA is for a particular property, it will take much longer to sell a $300,000 house in a $150,000 neighborhood, unless you drop the price significantly. Not impossible, of course, but it will take longer than normal to close, which is just as painful to your bottom line as selling well below market value.

While there are some exceptions, especially if the first three metrics are in your favor, as a general rule you want to stick to flipping houses valued within +/-25% of the neighborhood's average value.

5) What's the local spread between average listing price and average sale price in the last year? You could also use median listing price and median sale price over the last year, but the important thing is to make an apples to apples comparison. The goal is to make sure there's no large mismatch between listing prices and closing prices in the neighborhood.

There's always some variation between listing and closing prices and every market is different of course, but in general you want to see homes in that neighborhood selling within 5% of the asking price. If the spread is larger than 5%, then you should be skeptical of how accurate your comp and pricing models are. Now would be a good time to call up local listing agents and pump them for information. There's a good chance there's something about the local market that is affecting everyone's pricing. This is why I like to compare every estimate to recent sale comps from the local property appraisal's website. It may sound simple, but all the facts are laid out there, including the recorded deed and price. There is no source more accurate than an actual recording in the county, and it's free to boot.

Note: when evaluating home prices to determine equity, ignore pending home sales and only count the final sale price of recent comparable homes. Otherwise your data could be off by a wide margin.

However, when evaluating home prices to determine your listing price, pending home sales are quite important. Pending sales of comparable properties nearby, as in a sub-division, apartment/condo development block or particular neighborhood and not just in an arbitrary geographic distance, yield a wealth of useful and quite relevant information:

1) What is the average time on market for pending sales? This lets you estimate your holding costs better and decide if you should discount your price a little from the estimate appraised value. So far we've been using historical sales information to estimate this, but pending sales gives us the most up-to-date data.

2) Were there any reductions made to the initial listing price? If so, why?

3) Contact information for the listing agent working this deal, so I can pump them for information while the details are still fresh in their mind. This last part is quite important and doesn't mean you have to hire the agent.

Step 3: Contact listing agents from pending sales

Even if you have no plans to hire a real estate agent on a commission basis, there are other arrangements you can make. These pros have boots-on-the-ground insider knowledge of what's going on in a community market right this second, and you have a hot list of vetted leads in the local area, which is their bread and butter. A simple exchange of information is a win-win for both of you.

There are several ways you can approach them, but I prefer an old-fashioned phone call with a friendly but mutually beneficial conversation. I'll introduce myself and then give them a heads up about a new listing I might be getting in the same community and offer the exclusive right to show the property to their buyers first if they can answer some questions.

If I'm really scratching my head about what's going on in an area and they seem to be quite knowledgeable, I might even offer to send the agent a selection from my Excel sheet in exchange for a little more of their time. Those off-market, pre-foreclosure leads in the area that have some sizeable equity but not enough for me to act on them. The point is, I'm offering something of value that doesn't have to cost a dime.

It's rare that you don't have their enthusiastic attention at this point. Some of the most important questions to ask are:

- What's making nearby homes sell so fast/so slow?

- Why is there so much/so little inventory for sale in this area?

- How many of these places are getting multiple good offers?

- What specific features or property profiles are moving the fastest?

- What price do you recommend I list at and why? That doesn't mean we'll use this, since they're just coming up with a ballpark estimate at the moment, but if it's substantially below or above my current expected listing price, that's a red flag I've missed something. Could be a good thing or bad, but I don't want to be surprised either way when we go to market.

Step 4: Current Market Value Vs Long Term Home Value

It doesn't matter whether you plan to rent an investment out for years or flip it within weeks. Either way, you need an accurate estimate of the home's current-state value and the near future selling price before you buy the property. Don't fall prey to the temptation to just guesstimate the valuation based upon Zillow or some other broad metadata average.

Most definitely never follow the fantasy approach you see on TV or radio shows. Where they buy a property, renovate it the best they can and cross their fingers that the appraiser gives the place a high valuation.

In practice, there's a ton of "wiggle room" with appraisals. Regardless of how fancy the interior is, comparable nearby homes will always be the deciding factor in an appraisal. Especially when you're selling to retail buyers who need to take out a loan. If the house in question is too expensive for the area, the underwriters at the bank are going to keep ordering new appraisals until they get an estimate that they can live with.

Even if your appraisal is a pleasant surprise, if you're surprised in your investments, then you're doing something wrong. Of course there will be plus/minus margins of error in your estimates, but if you're ever truly blindsided by something, even in a good way, you made a mistake. You got lucky this time, but next time whatever you're missing might come back to bite you in the bum.

That all might sound quite simple, like elementary advice, but this little step of not confusing **market** value with **home** value trips up many professional agents and investors. Most set their selling price based upon the home's objective value, which assumes you have all the time in the world to wait for the very best offer. This doesn't always have a strong correlation to the actual current market value in a particular neighborhood, which is more heavily influenced by competition and recent/pending sales. They also often rely on gut feelings to tweak this selling price even further, which opens the door to all sorts of data-bias in even the most clear-headed investors.

To be fair, it took me a while to realize just how game-changing determining the current market value is, or how easy it is to use hard data to come up with a formula for setting a realistic selling price. Once I overhauled my entire evaluation and listing approach, everything changed. I cut my average time on market from 6 months to 4 for each property, and increased my yearly net returns from short-term flips from 20% to 30%... all just by changing how I crunched the numbers before listing.

And you can do the same thing if you stay focused on two key principles:

1) We want the estimated value that will likely be appraised by a seller's lender if they were to send an appraiser today. In other words, the current market value, to estimate our equity with accuracy. The

best way to get this number for off-market homes is to do your own unofficial CMA based upon the neighborhood's recent comp sales recorded at the property appraiser's office. You can use Corelogic Comps or some similar service for the initial equity screening, but you'll want to manually double check the appraisal through the local property appraiser's site before purchasing the property. We want to know exactly how much the home is worth right now, assuming we finish all basic repairs and get it up to an average selling condition.

The key is to not factor in any additional renovations, the exact opposite advice that you've probably heard many people give about creating an After Repair Value (ARV) price. That's a separate niche and requires too much speculation for our purposes, since we don't have enough data at the moment. You'll have to guess how this renovated property will be evaluated and compare the future result to a totally different set of comps, and then hope that the buyer's appraiser months down the road sees things your way. I don't know about you, but that's too many if's, and's or but's for my taste.

Now, I don't mean to belittle those brilliant rehabbers that can fix up and improve run-down properties for cheap and then resell at a premium. I admire anyone who can create new equity from nothing. It's just that's a rather advanced and high-risk niche, while I'm focused on teaching low-risk strategies that work in every type of market.

2) Once you have this estimated appraisal price, you then need to set a sell price that balances profit with speed.

Unless you have a buy, rent and hold long-term strategy, then you aren't interested in the best price you can get at some indeterminate point in the future, but rather the most realistic price you can fetch in the next few months. This has little to do with the home's value, but rather how cheap it is compared to the neighborhood, the home's curb appeal and the area's general appeal. In short, basic supply/demand principles like in any business.

Yes, this is why everyone cautions you to use the "70/30" rule or some other factor to make sure you have plenty of elbow room, but that's the source of many woes. They'll use this standard on the after repair value of the home, which is an idealized best-case scenario and generally higher than the short-term (less than six months) realistic sale price. Instead, the 70/30 rule should be applied to the discounted move-the-property-fast price.

For example, the traditional valuation approach might return a $200k ARV on an investment, with $10k in rehab costs. So you wouldn't spend more than $130k on the purchase. However, let's say the immediate neighborhood has many homes for sale at the moment, something that most CMA approaches don't take into account. With all this competition, the realistic price you can fetch in the short-run is only $180k.

Step 5: How To Set A Realistic Selling Price

Remember, a normal home seller can set the asking price at or even above the market value and just wait until they get an offer they're happy with.

For professional investors though, several other factors come into play that usually guarantees the market value and sell price will be different. Since direct holding costs, as well as indirect opportunity costs from missed investments pile up fast, you need to set a price that will move the property as soon as possible. Which isn't as painful as it sounds, since we're only investing in places with a ton of equity in the first place.

And while no, setting the listing price isn't an exact process, it's also not a complete game of guesswork either. There are plenty of hard rules you can follow to make sure your estimates don't veer too much into pessimistic territory and leave money on the table, or are too enthusiastic and keep you from closing fast. Now, I could write a whole book on this subject alone, and I do dedicate a few hours in my online course going over several real-world examples, but the core process is simple to understand.

I) Start with the market value (estimated appraisal value) that you also used to determine equity. Instead of using your gut to adjust the price by +/- percentage points based upon different property factors, we'll look at those comps in more detail and try to find some more on the property appraiser's site. We'll use those recent sales in the neighborhood to see how different factors affected the price of similar homes.

Note: When looking at these comps, it's better to go back in time rather than expand your geographic search area. Ideally, we'll find plenty of comparable homes sold in this neighborhood during the last 90 days—fresh data that should match current market conditions. However, if you can't find enough properties that are really comparable, it's better to look at nearby sales in the last 180 days or even last year before you expand your search into other neighborhoods.

The reason is quite simple: we can compensate for price differences between older and newer data samples in the neighborhood, the same data set, easier than we can between neighborhoods, which are totally different sets of data. For example, if we have to go back an entire year to find good comp sales close to our target investment, we can adjust for time by seeing how much average home values have risen or fallen in that area in the last year. If all homes in the neighborhood appreciated at 10% for the year, then we'll add 10% to the older comp's price to simulate a recent sale.

On the other hand, if we're looking at a recent comp from a different neighborhood more than a mile away, there are several X factors that we can't easily control for. Perhaps those places are farther away or closer to popular amenities, or an investor has gone on a buying spree there and driven up prices, or a sudden crime wave/pollution/traffic/construction issue is affecting local prices. You can't account for these statistical variations with the property appraiser's website and really need to talk to an agent who's working that beat to get the details.

II) Once you have the comps ready, the most important thing we're looking for is how fast can we move the property. This is determined by three factors. Each of which you'll use to increase or decrease your current market value as needed to arrive at your realistic selling price. Make sure you take them in order and cumulatively.

1) **Competition**.

This is the most often overlooked step. We want to look for comparable homes currently on the market, as well as pending sales.

With current sales, we're not so interested in their current list price as in the amount of inventory close to your target investment. The more similar homes for sale you find and the closer they are to your property, the more you're going to want to discount. Note: this does not mean you have to be the cheapest in the neighborhood, but that you should price a bit below your market value.

As mentioned before, pending sales of comparable properties yields a wealth of information, but at this step our primary concern is how much the pending price changed from listing. Yes, a small difference was likely caused by various credits to the buyer, but a significant (usually more than ~3%) difference is relevant for your pricing. If the contract price was higher than asking, the seller might have just hired a really good agent and received multiple offers. If the contract price is lower than asking, they might have been extra motivated to sell or simply priced too high to begin with.

This is valuable information we need to know to decide how much we should adjust our market value. That's why we want to contact the listing agent for every comp property where the contract price is significantly different than the listing and find out why. Only then can we decide whether we should follow suit and raise the price or drop it and save a ton of time on market.

2) **Time on market of recent sales.**

Add up and average the time it took to go under contract for all your comps, the same way you averaged their prices. You can then multiply this by your monthly holding (also called carrying) costs to quantify how much you can discount the house to make it move fast without cutting into your equity. As mentioned before, these holding costs are more than just insurance and property management fees. They also include the monthly increase to any mortgage payoff settlement.

For example, if the average comp sales time in the area was eight months and you'll have $1,000 in monthly holding costs, then you could lower your acceptance price by up to $6,000 for an immediate offer in the first month (also adding one month for closing). The $6k discount paid for itself without cutting into your profit margin.

Note: Cross check the sales history with the MLS to see if any of your comps were delisted and then relisted later. For a variety of reasons, this is a common practice. If so, add the time from all previous listings to your time on market estimate.

3) **Property's condition.**

a. Curb appeal. This is also the attractiveness or desirability of your property. It's highly subjective, of course, but there are several major features you can compare against your comps to see how they change the price.

For example, your investment has a waterside or park view, so look at just your comps with a similar feature and ignore those with a street view. Make a new average with those and subtract from the original comp price to get a rough approximation of the premium for this view. So if you arrived at a market value of $250k by looking at six very close comps, but the two that have a similar view are selling at $260k and $270k, then we can safely assume the view adds about $15k to the selling price and price accordingly.

Note: We're only looking at major features here that could add or subtract several thousand from the price. This is key to keeping everything realistic, since if we don't have enough data or can't discern a clear difference because there are many factors at play, then we should not consider a particular feature in our price estimate. That might sound complicated, but it's pretty straightforward in practice.

For example, say you're noticing that all your comps have great professional looking landscaping, but your property

123

seems bland. Not in bad shape, just not as pretty as everyone else. There's really difficult to objectively measure, so you won't consider it in your pricing estimate.

b. **Time and cost to rehab.** The direct costs of rehabbing your property with repairs and minor renovations is simple enough. Where things get complicated is comparing the value generated from these projects with the opportunity cost of putting in the bare minimum time and money to close as many deals as possible.

This is why we strive to avoid poor quality real estate and stick to the properties that need as little TLC as possible. Of course, that's not always possible in the real world, so it's important to run any additional renovation costs, above the minimum needed to get the home in a livable and sellable, against the value of just pricing lower and selling quicker.

Remember that you can always price low at an "as is" condition, and raise the price in stages as you improve the property. So use your renovation costs as an automatic discount on the sell price, and raise the price every month as you add new value.

For example, one of the cheapest yet highest value-adding renovations is replacing worn flooring with fresh laminate and then give everything a nice wax finish. I generally try to do this with any property I'm purchasing that's more than a couple of years old. Naturally, my partner has a project backload with all this constant work, but I'm not going to wait. I'll price the home as-is immediately at a 5-10% discount, and then remove that discount as soon as the upgrade is complete. I calculate the discount not from the estimated value the new flooring adds, but from my saved costs caused by not having to pay for the work and reduced holding costs from moving fast.

If someone comes along in the meantime and takes the property off my hands at that price, then great. Even at a lower profit on the deal, I can move on to the next investment and compound my returns. That's where the real value comes from.

Even if your niche centers around fixer-upper properties, then this evolving price structure is quite useful for you.

4) Putting it all together.

So, let's say my market value estimate came in at $200,000 for a new property. My minimum available equity threshold to enter this deal is 20% ($40k) and my running estimated equity tally at this point is $60,000. So far so good, but since home value and market value aren't the same, I still need to see if my realistic selling price will leave enough meat in the deal for me to bother sitting down at the table.

Now I'll go through the three price factors—competition, time on market and condition—to see if this is still a good deal.

Starting price: $200k.

- - $10k for competition. New price $190k. There are more than three comparable homes for sale in the same neighborhood, with list prices ranging from $195- $220. So we reduced price to be more competitive.

- + $5k from pending homes report. New price $195k. After looking at the inflated contract prices and talking with a few local agents, it appears this area is in high demand. Every property is getting multiple offers that raise the final price by $5-10k, so we use the lower end estimate to be conservative.

- - $6k from time on market. New price $189k. Despite the high demand, for some reason these properties are taking between 6-9 months to close. Agents you contacted believe it's caused by multiple lenders requiring multiple appraisals. My holding costs are $1,000 dollars a month, so I'll discount the initial price by six months of costs to help make sure we close within three months. If this doesn't happen by then, I can raise the price later.

- - $0 from property condition. My gut is telling me this home just has better curb appeal and could sell for a bit more than the nearby competition. However, I wasn't able to find any statistically significant proof in the recent sale comps. Since I'm not so familiar with this area and none of the agents I spoke to could quote me a dollar value for the small but special features of this home, I play it safe and make no change to my estimate.

The risk of underestimating the value by 1-2% is nothing compared to the risk of overpricing the house. Since in the first scenario the house will just sell faster, saving me money, whereas in the last things take longer and costs me money.

- - $5k in repair and rehab cost. The house is in pretty good condition and I could hold an open house as soon as the cleaning service is finished tidying up. However, there are a host of small issues that could add some serious value, such as replacing the gaudy carpeting, painting over all the multi-colored wall patterns in a simple white and replacing that ugly, mismatching stove and refrigerator. That'll all cost me $4k, plus another month in holding costs until my crew can finish.

- So my final price is $184k as is right now and $194k after rehab. In both cases, I have more than 20% available equity. Even at the lowest price, I still have 22% equity. If I have other potential deals but only enough capital for one, I'll compare the equity left over from the lowest offer to see which is the best deal.

- Only now, after sketching how the entire game will play out, am I finally ready to send the owner a hard purchasing offer.

Step 6: Title search and walk through with home inspector and lead contractor.

These are the standard pre-closing steps you'll do with every type of property.

Step 7: Off-Market Purchasing Contract Fundamentals

This does not have to be a convoluted process that requires many hours from your attorney. You can minimize risk and make sure all the bases are covered without spending a fortune on legal fees.

Afterall, for an investor, there are four things that matter the most:

1) Close fast before another cash investor comes along and drives up the price.

2) Get the tenant moved out in a quick and orderly manner.

3) Keep the home in the same condition it was when you conducted the walk through.

4) Make sure every provision serves as an exit clause, so you can walk away from the deal at the last second if you discover any nasty surprises or the seller isn't honoring the terms. On the same token, it should go without saying how important it is for you to stick by what you're promising.

The specific names of the forms can vary across all the different local courthouse jurisdictions, and whether or not certain items are included as provisions to the side agreement or separate contracts, so again, always double check with your lawyer that everything is in order for your local area.

The ultimate goal is to get the homeowner to sign a quit-claim deed, which simply transfers their interest in the property to you.

You'll accompany this with a side agreement (the contract) that includes any custom provisions you like. Make sure you include an explicit "arm's length transaction" disclosure signed by both parties. Naturally, everything needs to be witnessed, notarized and recorded per your state's requirements. I have sample forms on my website (www.lirankoren.com) that you can download to see how everything works in practice.

At a minimum, you want to include the following provisions:

1) General agreement to convey deed and transfer the homeowner interests to the buyer.

2) Auction surplus right's assignment from the homeowner to the buyer.

3) A structured payment plan instead of just a lump sum payment. For example, we will pay the homeowner $5k for

the deed immediately, and $10k when they move out within 30 days and leave the property in the same condition as it is now. Include a writ of possession clause to expediate eviction if necessary. Obviously, that's something we want to avoid at all costs, since it's unpleasant for everyone involved. Usually you can negotiate with the tenants, even offer a little extra moving money instead of just calling the sheriff, and this gives you more leverage in those situations.

4) Also specify in as much detail as you can in the provisions exactly what you mean by the property's condition and what will happen in the event the homeowner will not leave or the property's condition changes for the worse. For example, "Seller must leave appliances and landscaping features in place and not remove any fixtures."

5) Optional: If you're conducting a lease-back arrangement with the owner, include a month-by-month rental agreement. Bear in mind that statistically, most of these leases won't last more than a few months before the tenants stop paying. So you'll need an incentive to get the occupants out in an orderly manner. One thing that helps is to offer to pay the renter's security deposit out of your own pocket, which is budgeted on your end against what you would have paid for the title transfer payment. The owner can receive this "free" money only if they leave the property in the same condition as specified in the contract.

6) Optional: If you're just interested in the owner's surplus at auction, also include a general agreement to litigate on behalf of the homeowner for this property. You don't strictly need this, but it can help with some types of litigation. Again, double check with your attorney for the details of local law.

With that said, you don't want to make these agreements too complicated. We're looking for a fast "1, 2, 3" transaction. They should be able to read through the contract in minutes and have few, if any, questions. Then we can hand them a cashier's check before they leave the office and activate the agreement before any 3rd party slows things down. The goal is to sign, pay and record the quitclaim at the courthouse on the same day. And a big part of meeting that goal is keeping the homeowner from having second thoughts or any other worries.

So skip the typical legalese involving convoluted nested clauses riddled with Latin phrases. Use short sentences in plain English that anyone can understand. The simpler you keep the paperwork, the more confident the homeowner is with saying yes. Not to mention, how can someone comply with provisions they don't understand?

Foreclosure Auctions – No More Pyrrhic Victories

The next best hidden equity trail is foreclosure auctions. Yes, competition will be much stiffer since there are so many bidders, but we already have an ace up our sleeve.

By employing the same infrastructure you used to find the Lis Pendens for distressed homeowners, you can now scour the upcoming foreclosure notices for the next week. Pull their case numbers and cross reference with the property appraiser's site just like in the previous chapter. This will be even easier, since you won't have to estimate so many expenses or find and contact the homeowner. You can automate even more of the grunt work and focus your energy on conducting detailed comp reports and estimated resell price on the hottest picks.

We're scanning every single item coming up on the auction circuit for the next week, and not just a couple of things that we found interesting. That's what average investors do, and that's why they see only average returns.

Just like with pre-foreclosures, we know the equity in every single item before the opening bell. I cannot overstate how crucial that edge is. However, before we can start bidding, we need three further pieces of information:

1) Contact the attorney's office listed in the case history to learn out the opening bid ahead of time. Then rerun your equity estimate with that as the minimum acquisition cost to filter out the low-equity leads.

2) Make sure the party foreclosing is indeed the first lien holder. This might be obvious by looking at lien type, but not always. You'll be surprised how often a second mortgage lender or HELOC lender forecloses before the original mortgage. This is usually as simple as manually searching the court records for the defendant's name and seeing what other cases they have against them, and finding out which was filed first.

3) Due to the unknown title risks—we won't do an official title search until we've won a bid to keep costs reasonable—you need to budget a little bit more safety room in your maximum bid. Set your own risk tolerance, I use 30% estimated equity, but whatever you choose stick to it.

Once you have that information and sorted out all the leads, you can set up your watchlist and it's off to the races. I go through dozens of real-world examples in my online courses, but really that's all the key items.

The more you participate at auctions, the more you practice, the better feel you'll get for the pace of bidding and can outsmart other investors. But as long as you're doing the same equity and comp research as with distressed homes and stick to your max bid without getting emotional, you can't go wrong. You'll always have a major advantage over the other players.

I know that sounds boring, but it all comes down to data gathering and being organized, prepared and disciplined.

To recap those fundamentals:

1) Much like with pre-foreclosures, your first goal is to determine how much potential equity there is in the property.

This is where data mining comes in handy. Instead of picking a single auction or two that matches your interests, you can set the specific parameters of what you want to bid on and let your software search and download properties matching that profile. Then you weed them down for the best potential deals.

It's still important to read through the case history for auction sales, even though you know what happened. Some of the key insights you're looking for are:

- Any last-minute motions filed by the defendant that haven't been ruled on yet. We want to minimize the risk of a contested sale, so we're looking for places that the owner has given up on.

- Does the owner or any other tenant still live in the property? Ideally, you'll want to do a drive-by of the property first, but if time doesn't permit, the case history can give you a clue if you're going to have to evict someone and potential suffer damage to the property. If the defendant's mailing address or the address of any recent summons was delivered to the property address, then they're probably still living there.

- Purchasing a home through an auction clears out all known lien holders' interest, but that doesn't guarantee the property is free of all debt. So an extensive title search is necessary before you make final payment. For example, the new buyer is almost always responsible for any overdue property taxes or local building code violations. There may even be unknown notices of default that were filed after the auction was set.

- And if you're operating in one of the 16 or so "super lien" states, the home owner's association can foreclose independently of other lenders to recover unpaid dues. So double check for those liens.

Fast due diligence

Once you win the bidding, you'll have to place an immediate deposit. Every county has slightly different time frames between winning a bid and having to put up the full payment, but it's usually less than 24 hours. This is your last chance to do your due diligence and make sure you're getting a good deal, and it's always a short window.

- Conduct the most detailed professional title check you can. Also call up the local code enforcement and see if there are any fines assessed against the property.

- Have your attorney double check the case history to make sure you haven't missed anything.

- Talk to your realtor contacts who work in that area to get an idea of any special challenges in the neighborhood.

- Make sure the neighborhood doesn't have any lease restrictions if you're planning on renting.

After you've checked all these boxes, then rerun your equity estimate and make sure you're above water before making final payment. Since you budgeted a 30% cushion, it would take some huge surprises to scuttle the deal, but this is your last chance to cover your butt.

The Keys To Bidding And Winning At Auction:

1) Remember: winning an auction has nothing to do with getting the property, but rather getting it at the right price. This is especially true for auctions where the opening and/or max bid is hidden. The investor who knows what the home is worth and knows exactly how much they're willing to pay will win… even if they aren't the highest bidder.

2) Go all in or don't waste your time. If you've seen the property and have done your homework, and you know this is the deal you want to do, then make sure you put in your maximum allowed offer as the bid and go do something else. Don't look back. If you win, great. If you lose, then move on. Either way, never doubt yourself and change your bid.

3) I know, it might seem like you're leaving money on the table. Why not place 90% of your max bid and then monitor the auction and keep raising until you hit your max offer level?

4) Very simple: your time is better spent researching new deals. The marginal improvement to your bottom line for shaving off an extra one or two percent in the bid price is nothing compared to the money you could make doing research into the next deal. There's always going to be someone with a higher risk tolerance and more cash burning a hole in their pocket than you. Your only edge is your ability to learn more about the property by coming up with an accurate final sale price and figuring out ways to unlock equity in the home. That's your advantage over the "big boys," so stick to what you do best and let the billion-dollar funds fight bidding wars. While they're busy squabbling over the hottest deals, you're

quietly plugging away, doing your homework, and amassing a vast inventory of smaller but more lucrative properties they didn't have the time to investigate.

Even in the current bull market, there are plenty of other auctions to bid on. Granted, with auctions you won't have the time to do a home inspection first and contractor walkthrough, so there's more guesswork involved, but once you've made your guess, treat your estimates as Holy Scripture. Any X factors, such as knowing that homes in a certain neighborhood will sell above market value, should be factored in to your equity estimate and max bid. Once you start bidding, your numbers must be set in stone.

For example, if you're convinced you can move this house in short order for $200k and you're using a 30% standard for setting your max bid tolerance, then your max bid is $140k. Not 139k or 141k. This is easier when the bids are hidden, of course, but it gets harder when bids are open. When you've been the highest bidder all day... and some random person comes along one minute before the auction closes and drops a $140,500 bid. I know how tempting it is to say, "Well, selling for $200k was my conservative estimate. There's some wiggle room, and I really need to increase my inventory, so let me up the bid just a smidgen..."

Don't fall for the old trap of second-guessing your estimates and increasing your bid "just a little." In the heat of the moment, with the timer ticking down, it's too easy to rationalize any reckless action.

I've been there. I know that's easier said than done, but just push away from the table and think big picture. Even when bids are hidden, you can get carried away. You've placed your best bid and you're the top bidder...until the last 20 seconds before the auction closes. Then suddenly the red label disappears from your position.

You're no longer the top bidder.

Perhaps the bank just upped the ante by a measly $100 to try and squeeze a bit more out of your bid. Or maybe another investor outbid you by $10k. Either way, you have seconds to decide if you should up your bid. It's just a small margin, right? Shame to miss out on a deal now just because we drew an arbitrary line in the sand. Your money isn't doing any good rusting away in the bank. Besides, there's no real way to know exactly how much equity is in there until I do a title search and walk through with my partner. It's all just an estimate right now...

That's precisely why you should stick to your max bid. That excessively pessimistic estimate of available equity is your only safety margin to make sure you turn a profit. So step away from the deal and go bid on something else. You can't win them all, but at least you haven't lost anything. Remember, auctions have more uncertainty than pre-foreclosure deals. There's statistically a higher chance of finding big problems with the title or property condition, since the home has been in arrears for so long. And you won't know about this until after you drop a non-refundable deposit and inspect the property.

So if you don't stay disciplined and let a little emotion seep into your bidding, you'll wind up with a Pyrrhic victory that makes you wish you'd lost the auction.

Home Owners Association Foreclosure – The Safe But Lucrative Way To Enter These Positions

Note: To be crystal clear, I'm not advocating rent/equity skimming or anything along those lines. I'm talking about legally and ethically profiting from priority of liens. You must always check with a local foreclosure attorney that you're complying with the law. With that said, many jurisdictions allow exceptions to rent skimming conditions to protect homeowners and investors from predatory lending practices. This allows you to legally collect rent or the equivalent if you follow a very specific checklist of actions and meet certain criteria. So talk to a local attorney to learn your rights as an investor.

Profiting from HOA Liens and HOA Foreclosures

This is where the waters get muddy for many new investors and even some seasoned ones. To be fair, the whole system confused me for a while, which is why I stayed out of this niche until I could wrap my mind around the intricacies. Yes, it's exciting how in super lien states you can gain cheap title to expensive properties for a song. But that's only the beginning. There are two huge caveats to keep in mind:

1) This is a "dirty" title. The property still has all the former financial obligations and other debt holders can still foreclose later. That's why the opening bid is so cheap.

2) Don't try to "get ahead" of the game by buying HOA liens before the auction has begun. Yes, in a super lien state the HOA has priority interest… assuming they file their Lis Pendens first. Otherwise, the standard "First in time, first in right" applies. Meaning if anyone else simply records their lawsuit one second before you, then they "win" and it's game over for you.

I've lost count of how many times I've seen people way overbidding on HOA auctions, or even worse, purchasing the HOA lien after another lender filed a Lis Pendens and losing their entire investment. All because they read that first part of the law and ignored the fine print. They could have made more money with less risk by just dumping their cash into scratch off lottery tickets.

136

Now before I scare you off, let me give you an example of how lucrative this niche can be if you take your time. I bought a beachside condo that's my favorite personal vacation getaway by using the HOA foreclosure to find the underwater homeowner well before his lender began foreclosing. It was worth $650k back in 2014, with the poor homeowner facing a $700k mortgage. I helped him out and picked it up for a total of $27k, including $15k to the HOA to make them withdraw their Lis Pendens. My lawyer is still running circles around the original out of state mortgage lender to this day.

Obviously, this approach involves extensive legal maneuvering and attention to detail. For example, if you bought the HOA lien or any other lower level lien after a higher priority lien holder, such as the original mortgage owner, filed a Lis Pendens, then your interest will be 100% wiped out later. You'll have no standing to challenge the foreclosure, since you aren't named as a defendant in the lawsuit.

You'll be surprised how often investors make this avoidable mistake. I see individual investors buying into such weak positions all the time. Quite often, they actually did check to see if a Lis Pendens was filed and found none, but they didn't follow up on the case history every day. By the time they negotiated a payoff with the lien holder and recorded the sale, the mortgage lender had already recorded their Lis Pendens... so the investor lost all their money simply because they got sloppy. On the plus side, since they're paying off the property's debt, they're creating free equity for the next investor that comes along and carefully reads the case history.

There's even a way to take advantage of this niche and gain controlling interest in the property after the foreclosure process has begun. Yes, once the Lis Pendens is filed, the underwater homeowner is the defendant, so you can't "get inside" the case and become the indispensable party. However, that doesn't mean the homeowner has to fight the case. You can buy the "assignment of rights" to the defendant's case, allowing you to litigate the lawsuit on their behalf.

So before you take advantage of HOA liens, you need to know exactly when and how to enter and precisely what your exit strategy is.

1) How to keep from overbidding

Just like with any investment, you need to carefully read all the public records, legal case histories and the property's tax records to determine the minimum level of debt outstanding. Known liens don't always include a final judgment on other assessed costs, like interest and attorney's fees. Plus, at this fairly early stage when the bank hasn't foreclosed yet, you can expect that not every potential stakeholder has yet filed a formal lien claim. So you need to add a larger margin of error to that debt load than you would when bidding on lender-foreclosures. I usually double my normal debt estimate when calculating the equity spread, and subtract that from the most conservative estimate of the property's market value. Only then should you apply your 70/30 or other risk tolerance factor to determine your max bid.

So at first glance, that $5,000 HOA judgment being auctioned off on a $200,000 house with only $120,000 outstanding on the first mortgage and no other liens seems like a good opportunity. Especially during the adrenaline rush of an auction. You might be tempted to just add a quick 10% to the mortgage lender's balance, toss in the $5k HOA judgment and think you could bid up to $23k on the property and still stick to your 30% rule.

But take a moment to consider how risky that is. Just like with foreclosure auctions, there's so much you don't know until you finish a complete title search, so it pays to be pessimistic. For example, even if there are no big surprises, what if you're in one of those states that gives the homeowner a long redemption period to buy back the home? In some states, this can be as long as six months. If the home's not vacant, you can expect delays and extra costs from evicting tenants. And of course, if your legal team isn't in-house, you can expect your attorney costs to snowball before you're done.

Most of all, you need to factor in the opportunity cost of paying off any other debt before you can sell. Since you don't have a clean title, it can be incredibly difficult for prospective buyers to qualify for financing. So instead of paying off the bank with the proceeds of a sale, like with pre-foreclosure flips, you have to put up the money to clear the title first. Funds that could be working somewhere else.

Once you take all this into account, you'll see why you need a larger than normal equity spread to justify buying the HOA judgment at auction. Which is not to say that you can't find some great deals out there. I've closed on a dozen of these auctions in just my local county during the last year, but you should only bid on the most lucrative opportunities. It really is easy to overbid on these "cheap" properties, since even savvy investors can lure themselves into believing what they want to see in their research. But as long as you build in extra caution into your estimates, you'll avoid the costly mistakes so many investors are making every single day.

2) Purchasing the HOA note after a Lis Pendens is filed.

This is the costliest mistake you can make, but the easiest to avoid. Yet it's still almost as common as overbidding. Yes, buying the HOA judgment at auction *or* going directly to the distressed owner in pre-foreclosure are cheap ways to gain controlling interest in a property… But that's only if you purchase the HOA note *before* any lien holder files a Lis Pendens. If you buy into the position after any party files a Lis Pendens, then you won't be listed as a defendant and you will lose all of your investment. This might sound simple, but it's a regular mistake that I come across in so many of the case histories I'm studying on a daily basis.

From talking with new clients, the confusion seems to rest with not quite understanding what they're purchasing with an HOA lien and the priority of liens. Regardless of when you're buying the HOA note, you're only buying the HOA's interest in the property. You do receive legal title, but it's a "dirty title." It doesn't matter if you're operating in a "super lien" state, like Florida. You're still obligated to the home's other liens. This is completely different from a lender foreclosure auction, where every other party's interest is cleared out in the process of foreclosing.

This is where so many investors run into trouble. They forget that gaining the quitclaim deed from the owner is the most important part of the process. The HOA lien just gives us a foot in the door. So, the two pre-auction points when you could theoretically purchase the HOA's interest to gain title to the property, though the risk is through the roof:

1. **When the HOA has filed a lien but not yet a Lis Pendens for foreclosure.**

   This is what so many people try to do, but they run into trouble far too often. They think if they move fast and negotiate a deal with the HOA and homeowner to get the deed and rights assignments, they can position themselves to profit from any lender foreclosure auction surplus. Or even outbid everyone else at auction and gain clear title much cheaper, since any surplus over the lender's judgment would go to them.

   I can't stress enough how incredibly risky this strategy is. The problem is this all could take weeks to arrange, and you have no idea how close the lender is to foreclosing. Maybe they're months away; maybe the paperwork is already in the mail. Even if you conducted a full title search and found no other Lis Pendens recorded, the lender could file one at any minute, which would wipe your investment out.

   Remember, since you don't yet have the deed, you won't be listed as a defendant. The only interest in the foreclosure proceedings you'll have is for the original lien that you already bought, and that's assuming there is a surplus after the first judgment is paid off. So the best case scenario you can hope for is to break even. It's quite likely you'll lose everything you put into the position. The only solace you can expect is maybe a fruit basket from the lender thanking you for paying off part of the property's debt and making them richer.

2. **When the HOA has received a final judgment but not yet gone to auction.**

   Here, the HOA has filed a Lis Pendens and received a final judgment award from the court, but the original mortgage lender has not yet filed their own Lis Pendens. At this point, a date in the near future has been set for the auction, but it hasn't begun yet. Now I don't recommend this as a buying opportunity even if does seem less risky to enter the position now.

It doesn't matter what's going on with this case, since you can have multiple foreclosures going on simultaneously. You're still racing the bank to position yourself as the title owner. They can even file a Lis Pendens while you're in the middle of an HOA foreclosure auction, wiping out the interest of anyone who comes into the position later. Another great example why title searches or so crucial before making final payment, by the way.

Instead, if the auction date is coming up, you can skip paying off the HOA judgment and just buy the deed and assignment of surplus rights straight from the homeowner. Then you can profit from any auction surplus or pay off the HOA before the auction and start selling or renting out the house before the lender has even begun foreclosing.

With that said, there is a simpler and safer way to profit from properties saddled with HOA liens.

3) Go after just the surplus

While I generally recommend getting the quitclaim deed from the homeowner just like in a distressed property sale, and then paying off the HOA to stop the foreclosure, there is another option. If you aren't interested in owning the property, but you expect a large spread between the lender's foreclosure judgment and how much the home will sell at auction for, then you can position yourself to profit from that expected surplus.

For example, if you see a home valued at $350k, with a $250k mortgage and a $5k HOA final judgement attached, but no Lis Pendens filed yet, you can go straight to the HOA and buy their judgement and rights to surplus. With a little research into the case history to make sure the HOA has the legal rights to surplus assignment, you can bypass the homeowner and just wait for the auction. In my experience, a property like this, even if the property is underwater with the mortgage, should go for at least $25k at auction. So that's a tidy surplus in my pocket.

If you're the risk-taking type, you can even play with your position and bid against yourself, through another entity. All you do is wait for the auction to come, monitor it and make sure the difference between the judgement and the actual bid is good enough for you to make a profit. Then keep topping the latest bid by a little bit. If you overshoot, oh well. Then the position is a wash. If someone comes along and tops you, well, all the better.

Sure, you don't have any further interest in the property, but you made a quick and sizeable profit with a bare minimum of investment. Remember, to pull this off you need:

- To know who will have priority for the surplus and what is the expected amount.

- A good idea of how much it will sell at auction.

4) Negative equity – Using HOA to profit from underwater owners

Usually it's more difficult to profit from underwater homes when scanning Lis Pendens from lenders, because you'll have little standing to fight the bank after they've filed their lawsuit. However, the HOA auction gives us a unique opportunity to enter the position real cheap ahead of the bank.

We're still conducting the standard title transfer from the homeowner tactic, but we're doing it before a Lis Pendens is filed so we become the indispensable party. Then we'll negotiate an HOA payoff to stop that foreclosure, while fighting the lender's foreclosure as soon as they get involved. Now we can delay the sale and rent the property out, then settle the debt at an incredible rate or just buy the place back at auction. But again, that's only if you also get the title transfer from the homeowner as well, and do so before the lender forecloses.

In many cases, this is also the cheapest way to purchase the HOA foreclosure because there's far less competition.

For example, there's a $5,000 HOA Final Judgement Auction foreclosure. The house is worth $250,000. No Lis Pendens is filed yet. Mortgage owed is about $350,000.

When I see a $5k judgement by HOA with no Lis Pendens started at auction. As an investor I want it, because I know there are so many ways I can eke out more equity. However, so does everyone else. This has become a particularly hot trend since 2015.

So why spend $25k - $35k at auction, when I can look up the case # and property address, then skip trace the owner. I could get the deed and surplus assignment direct from the underwater owner for likely only $10k and earn several times as much before it goes to auction.

But let's explore all your opportunities here, even in a worst-case scenario. Let's say a $200k home has a $10k HOA lien against it, plus a $300k mortgage. And that's just the debt you spotted in the unofficial title search. If they're that deep underwater, likely they aren't paying the property taxes, insurance and who knows what else.

Well, don't run away quite yet. There's a particularly sophisticated investor niche that can help these "hopeless" homeowners. The owner has clearly abandoned this house and thinks he can only lose money on the property. Which means any cash deal you offer him would seem like a dream come true.

But why the heck would you throw a penny into a property that has -50% equity? Because if you're fast enough to buy and record the title *before* a Lis Pendens is filed by any other lien holder, you have a huge advantage. As the title holder, you become an "indispensable party" to the home… but without any obligations to the lender. After all, you didn't sign any promissory notes. Now, this doesn't mean the bank doesn't have an interest to the property, just that they can't remove your interest. So if they eventually sell it at auction, you're entitled to any surplus above their final judgement.

So you offer this homeowner $5k in cash to transfer the title to you. That's about 10,000% more than they ever expected to see from the house, so they're quite pleased. Then you pay off the $10k HOA lien so your title is completely clear. Boom, you just bought a $200k home for $15k, and don't owe a debt to anyone.

Eventually, the lender will notice the title transfer and sue for foreclosure, with you named as the defendant. That process alone takes several months, depending on where they are in the foreclosure process, but it's no big deal. There are so many ways to fight this and buy more time. Any halfway decent lawyer can file motion after motion to keep the wolves at bay for at least two years. Mine specializes in this field and can usually fight them off for three years… all while I'm renting the place out at a fat profit, since I'm not paying a mortgage on the property. All I'm paying for are the HOA fees and the normal property management and landlord expenses.

Now, for obvious ethical and legal reasons, you need to disclose these facts to your renters. Even better, you should stick to short-term, Airbnb type rentals to avoid problems.

And that's assuming the lender is fully committed to auctioning off the property. Quite often, the bank realizes how long I can fight this, how uncertain home values are in the future and understands the time and opportunity costs involved. So if I want to, I can always negotiate a "short payoff settlement" at a steep discount to get the mortgage forgiven.

Of course, if there's significant equity in the home or rental rates in the area aren't so high, I don't want to rent it out. I want to sell fast. So it's more profitable for me to not fight the foreclosure nor negotiate a payoff. Instead, I'll do everything I can to speed up the foreclosure process for the lender. Because once this goes to auction, I have two huge advantages over every other bidder. First, since I have physical access to the property while every other investor can only do a drive-by, I can put together a much more accurate CMA and rehab cost estimate. Second, I can outbid everyone else, because everything over the bank's final judgement will be returned to me.

For a common example from a past deal, I bought the deed for a home valued at $250k direct from a distressed home owner. After paying off all the lower level liens, like the HOA and some unpaid taxes, I wound up investing ~$17k into the property. A week later, the mortgage lender notices what's going on and files their Lis Pendens to start foreclosure, naming me as the sole defendant.

My original plan was to fight the bank and rent the place for at least two years, since the property was near a university and could charge a hefty rental premium. It should have been easy to double my investment even after land lording costs. However, once the home inspector submitted his report and my partner did a thorough walk-through, we realized the house wasn't nearly as well maintained on the inside as it appeared from the street. Well, "maintained" is a cute way to put. Clearly the last owners were not pleased with their bank and took vengeance in those final days before they moved out. I mean, what were they ever going to do with those PVC pipes they ripped out of the walls? But I digress. In short, it would take at least two months and another $40k to fix up the extensive damage the previous occupants left. So the home was definitely over-valued at the moment.

Rather than disappointed, I was excited to find out this new information that no else knew about. You see, the bank was suing for $130k, plus interest and expenses. The mortgage had only been in arrears for three months, so if they foreclosed fast, their total claim should have only come to $143-150k. If I fought them for two or three years though, they'd likely get a final judgment that would exceed the home's value.

So I contacted the surprised loan servicer and instead of pitching a cash-for-keys deal or making any legal threats, I simply asked how I could help expedite the foreclosure process. What did they need from me and my lawyer to make the process go smoother and faster? A few months later, they got the house up for auction, with a final judgement of $152k. Even though I could have outbid everyone with my surplus position, I didn't even bother placing a bid.

There just wouldn't have been enough equity in the house to make it worth my time after paying off the lender, shelling out for the expensive repairs, plus my original investment and holding/closing costs. But I did monitor the sale, curious if the surplus alone would net me a profit. Just as I expected, plenty of investors were drawn to the large spread between the judgment amount and estimated value. Those investors sticking to the 70/30 rule were placing ~$170-180k bids, depending on how they calculated the home's value. Even had a short bidding war in the last few minutes, which drove up the final auction sale price to $185k.

And that extra $33k surplus between the judgement and final sale price? Deposited in my account a few weeks later. Grand total return of about 50% on my initial investment within two months, all without spending a dime on renovation or closing costs. So, no, I have no regrets about buying "a lemon" house. If you do your equity homework, you can often turn them into lemonade.

Had things turned out otherwise and the house was in great condition, it still would have been profitable to push for the foreclosure. Since everything over the final judgment amount would be returned to me, I could have easily outbid the competition and purchased the home free and clear for the net price of $152k (minus foreclosure fees). Which would have unlocked almost 40% equity in the property before even doing a thing to rehab the place.

These strategies might sound exotic, but they're quite routine. I've taken title to over 100 properties, especially condos, using this technique. The oldest dates back to 2013, and we're still renting it out just for the cost of HOA fees, taxes and standard property management fees. The relatively minor initial cash investment means I'm usually earning 300% or more. It's not only a great place to park excess cash when I'm in between larger deals, but pretty much my standard method nowadays for accumulating rental inventory. There's no cheaper or faster way to rent out high quality properties at such a steep premium.

5) Renting out properties in foreclosure

As long as you are the title owner you can legally rent the house out. Obviously, there are a few extra conditions you need to check off to avoid trouble:

- Keep paying the HOA fees and property taxes as long as you have a renter in there. All other liens and debt collectors you can ignore or fight in court.

- Offer the tenants a month-to-month lease and treat them as well as you would any long-term renter. Make sure your property management agent explains quite clearly that this is an investment property being foreclosed on by a previous lender and there's a chance they might have to vacate the property early. Include some form of financial compensation to cover the tenant's unexpected movement costs if the bank forces the auction earlier than planned. Besides basic human decency, doing all of this will increase the quality of your renters and keep you from getting a reputation as some sort of "slum lord."

- In the unlikely event that the lender tries to levy your rent income while in foreclosure, don't worry. This is easy for any foreclosure attorney to parry. It's rare they try this for residential rents, since the profit margins for them after attorney fees are so low. This is mostly a scare tactic intended to bring you to the bargaining table.

6) Fighting the foreclosure

I should write a whole book on this subject alone. Yes, I've learned plenty of tips working with some of the best foreclosure attorney's in my state, plus discovered a few unique legal tricks myself. And I do cover this legal maneuvering in more detail in my online courses, but the problem is so much of the specific process varies from state to state. Even sometimes county to county. The names and filing order of certain motions, how many days you have to file specific petitions, etc—the details vary in each jurisdiction.

I realize this all sounds intimidating and needlessly complex at first glance, but if you're working with a reliable attorney who specializes in foreclosure litigation, you'll learn the ropes in a hurry. The potential rewards, and lack of competition, is why it's well worth investing the time and money to master this niche. Here's the broad stroke overview of foreclosure litigation when your goal is simply to delay the auction as long as possible:

Early game:

Here you've assumed title, either from an HOA auction or direct purchase from the homeowner. You're either leasing the property back to the original owner or you've found a new tenant on a month-to-month lease. The original lender has not yet filed their Lis Pendens to start foreclosure.

Mid game:

You enter this stage when the first mortgage lender gets serious and files their Lis Pendens but has not yet received a final judgment.

End game:

Now the lender has a final judgment from the court and an auction date has been set. It's time for you to choose your exit strategy of profiting from the surplus, buying back the home or push for a last-ditch settlement. By this point, you've learned a lot more about the property after so many years of physical occupancy, so you should be able to come up with scalpel sharp equity estimates.

In either case, let your tenant know as soon as possible. Even after the auction, if you need to buy some more time for the tenant to move, you can file an objection to the sale. You'll rarely win at this point, but it does buy a few more weeks to make sure you're not violating the month to month lease agreement. If you have a quality tenant, this is obviously quite important. Maybe you can even move them into another property of yours if there's a vacancy.

PHASE THREE:
Risk Management In Any Market

Speed, Inventory And Opportunity Cost – Why A Scrawny Bird In The Pan Is Worth A Dozen In The Bush

If you're dreaming of flipping the perfect house and scoring the "big dirty," or plan to retire early from a handful of house flips, then let me spare you the pain and burst your bubble now. Retail real estate investing is much like regular retail—it's all about volume and inventory turnover. Amazon didn't grow from a humble used book retailer to a trillion-dollar company by selling expensive luxury brands. They focused on dominating the market for low margin products that they could sell fast and repeatedly to the masses. As a real estate investor, you need that same mindset to find continued success that builds upon itself.

You won't be buying and holding properties, like some old timey land speculator waiting on some grand future development. Nor are you going to renovate some shack into a mansion for Hollywood stars to gobble up.

Instead, if you're serious about not just surviving but thriving in this ultra-competitive business, then you're going to stick to the far less glamourous but safer classic strategies. That means buying as many boring, average-valued homes as you can, performing the bare minimum rehab and then flipping them for a modest profit as fast as possible. Rinse and repeat. No, it's not "sexy," but it's the only proven system that works in any type of market.

This approach is also the safest. Think about it. If no one deal can make you, no bad deal can break you.

Turnover

Ideally, you should aim for a four-month turnover, from placing your initial purchase bid to final closing when you sell. And do so with several houses at a time.

Inventory

In this business, there's no sense in sitting on a pile of cash for a rainy day. Yes, naturally, maintain a liquidity cushion to protect against any surprises, but put the bulk of your capital back to work as soon as you close a deal. You can rest on your laurels when you're ready to retire.

The Game Changing Power of Inventory Turnover

Let's say you're starting out with a $20,000 war chest. After cruising the court records, you snag a title transfer from a distressed homeowner on the verge of foreclosure and bankruptcy for $10k. There's another $100k in liens on the home. Even if you can't negotiate that debt load down, there's still some sizeable equity in the home at the moment.

So now you have a choice to make about how to maximize your profit. You realistically expect the house would move right now for $150k, with only regular staging and minor repairs. After clearing the debt and factoring in your total costs, you would net just $22,500, but do so in only 3-5 months.

However, let's assume renovation and rehab are your forte. Passion, really. You're quite confident if you pump in the rest of your cash, and plenty of your own elbow grease, you can flip this bad boy for $250k... but it will take all year. Despite the increased investment, holding and closing costs, you calculate that you would still net $67,500 when everything is said and done. Exactly as much as doing the other faster flip three times a year, so why not focus on just this house?

The problems are those compounding returns and missed opportunity costs. If you stuck to the quicker but less profitable option, you'll have twice as much working capital for your next investment ($42,400 versus $20,000). This allows you to purchase more expensive properties with higher equity or replicate a similar flip as the first time…but do two of these deals at once.

For the sake of simplicity, let's say you put your capital to work building up inventory and your next investments are two different houses priced the same. You earn $20,000 from one but had some unforeseen problems with the second so only made $10,000 profit there. Still, you've grown your initial $20,000 nest egg into $72,400. And there's still four months left in the year… So you put all that cash into flipping four properties at once this time. The first two generate $20k in profit each, the next $30k, your best deal yet. Let's even say at this point you get a little overconfident and make a mistake. Grossly underestimated your costs or missed something in your market value analysis. So you actually lose $10k on the fourth deal. Stings a little, but you aren't frazzled.

Because when you add up the balance sheet at next year's tax time and take stock of the year, you can barely sit still. Instead of busting your butt all year to turn around one great flip for only $67,500, you flipped seven boring properties in a single year and earned $102,400. Even after getting hosed on one deal and never earning more than 20% on a single endeavor. Now, instead of massaging lotion into your bruised and calloused hands, you're popping open champagne while strategizing how to flip twice as many homes next year.

Home Rehab –
Adding Maximum Value With Minimum Effort

What improvements and repairs are actually worth the expense?

You won't see me go into much detail here, because you're probably getting sick and tired of hearing it. Stick to simple, generic and fast improvements that make the property look "nice" but not special. Unless you have a unique advantage and your niche is rehabbing seriously damaged properties, then you should be rejecting any investment that requires a significant repair budget during the inspection and walk-through phase.

Remember, we're hunting for hidden value and ways to unlock equity. Few home improvement projects are going to add much more value than they cost, so the goal is simply to get the home into a saleable shape as cheaply and quickly as possible.

Maybe that $10,000 complete revamp of the kitchen or master bath you're thinking about could add $15,000 to the final sale price, but that's pure speculation. There's no accounting for the tastes of your prospective buyers. Even if you turn out to be right and everything works fine, the net return will be much less than 50%. You're adding expenses by holding onto the property longer and even worse, losing out on opportunity costs since you're tying up money that you could use elsewhere. And that's the *best-case* scenario when your bet pays off exactly as planned.

If you took to heart the previous lesson about the massive value of flipping as fast as possible to build up inventory and earn compound returns, then this should be an easy mindset to adopt. Every extra day you're holding onto a property should feel like someone's ripping money out of your pocket.

Note: With that all said, don't ever cut corners. Never give in to the temptation to ignore something that needs to be fixed in favor of painting over it or skipping the permitting process to save a few bucks. You're just shooting yourself in the foot. Besides the obvious costs when the buyer discovers these problems and demands expensive last-minute credits, or even backs out of the deal entirely, your reputation is on the line. Not just with future retail buyers, but investors and other pros you need on your side for long-term success. Nothing is going to hobble your business faster than getting a reputation as a sketchy, "fly by night" operator.

Nuts And Bolts Of Renovating And Managing Contractors.

Trust is good, but control is better.

The most time-consuming aspect of flipping any home is that you must micromanage everything that's going on at the property. Whether you're doing that yourself or you have a well-experienced general contractor as a partner, someone needs to inspect all the work that's being done with an eagle-eye. And on a regular basis.

Every project requires a different inspection schedule depending on its complexity, cost and risk. For example, you probably don't need to check every hour that the painters are doing a good job. Just popping your head in once to ask if they "want anything to drink," while glancing around to make sure they're using the right paint and spreading it evenly is enough.

On the other hand, for larger items like kitchen remodels or adding/removing walls, you should check in at different progress stages. At a bare minimum, you should come by at 25%, 50% and 75% complete levels. Take your time and compare the blueprints or installation instructions to what's in front of you. The final product might look nice, but if anyone cuts corners in the process and skips important details, you could find the project failing the code enforcement inspection, saddling you with more fees and headaches later.

So ask every question that pops in your head, no matter how minor or "stupid" they sound. The key thing is never wait until a big job is done, or even half-finished, before seeing the progress yourself. Even if there are no issues, these constant inspections aren't a waste of time. You'll sleep better at night, while learning invaluable lessons about the ins and outs of repairs and renovations. And not to put too fine a point on it, but your constant presence is a great motivator to keep your workers honest and focused.

The Only Dumb Questions Are The Ones Never Asked

Never be afraid to speak up and question anyone you're working with. This isn't offensive or pushy, but rather being proactive. A true professional won't get defensive nor make excuses for any mistake. They'll either patiently explain why you're mistaken, citing the relevant building codes of manual's instructions, or simply accept responsibility, fix the error fast and implement corrective measures to make sure it doesn't happen again. If for some reason your contractors bristle, get angry or make excuses while you are being civil and just asking questions, then that's a huge red flag you're working with amateurs and should find someone else.

It's your money and reputation that's on the line, after all. Perhaps you have no experience with plumbing, carpentry or electrical work, but you at least know how things should look. Anything slightly out of place to your untrained eye is a good sign there's something deeper wrong.

So never worry about speaking up and challenging your contractors about even minor errors. If they don't immediately repair the issue and make sure nothing like that happens again, it's time to fire them and find someone else. Now, everyone makes mistakes and good help is hard to find, so don't be too hasty. It's in your best interest to try everything you can to resolve the issue before pulling the plug, but if the contractor can only provide excuses instead of solutions, then the sooner you bail out the better. Yes, it's frustrating having to abandon a partially finished project and go through the hassle of finding another crew to finish... but it's always far cheaper to get things done right the first time. And the earlier in the process you pull the plug, the less money you lose.

Friends and family

Going hand in hand with control is the crucial need to never hire anyone you're close to. It's fine to partner with friends and family as equals, but hiring them to *work* for you is a recipe for disaster. Adding a personal relationship to the client/contractor relationship is just begging for trouble.

I know, I know. That's far easier said than done. Your cousin is good with his hands and really needs the work. Your sister-in-law just started a landscaping business and could use some initial clients. Your lover, old Army buddy, best friend since childhood, etc. is going through hard times and you own them big. The examples go on and on, and they all seem like win-win situations. What could be better than hiring someone you trust and being able to help out someone you care about at the same time?

Let's face the harsh reality though: far more things can go wrong by mixing personal affairs and emotions with business than can go right. And you're in the business of risk *management*, not in taking unnecessary gambles.

Even if you don't have to deal with a case of incompetence, laziness or someone overselling their skills, everyone still makes mistakes or has personal life issues that get in the way. What do you do when your son-in-law makes an honest mistake that requires expensive repairs? A pro contractor that you aren't related to would fix the problem at their own cost, but what are you supposed to do with family? Are you going to make him work "off the clock," basically taking money out of your family's pocket to fix things? Or just take the financial hit yourself? Maybe you should fire him and get someone else? There's no happy outcome in this situation, so do yourself and your loved ones a favor by not putting anyone in this predicament in the first place.

Now, I'm not saying you have to be a cold-hearted SOB and tell them to go to hell. In this business, you'll make all sorts of contacts in short order with other investors, contractors and property management firms. If your friend or family member really has some skill, then recommend them to your colleagues. Freelancers live or die by word of mouth recommendations, and trust is notoriously hard to come by in this world, which means a few good words speaks volumes.

So if you genuinely care about someone, do them a real favor and help them get work with anyone but you.

Preemptive Negotiating –
How To Keep The Upper Hand Even In
Any Market.

It all comes down to leverage, of course, but leverage is not a clear-cut "you have it or you don't" situation. Both the buyer and seller bring all sorts of pressure against each other in every deal, so leverage is a matter of degree. Naturally, you know you need to minimize every pressure point the other side has on you, while maximizing your own pressure, to get a leverage advantage.

However, an even better approach is to structure your operations so that the other party never has a chance to apply any significant leverage in the first place. In short, stack the negotiating deck in your favor before you even meet with sellers or buyers.

This isn't as hard as it might sound. The key is to identify the specific pressure points the other party could bring to bear and maneuver around them well in advance. So let's go over the most powerful sources of supposed leverage your clients, tenants and prospective buyers have over you, and how you can nip those threats in the bud... and turn them to your advantage.

Shopping your offer to create a bidding war

This is only leverage if you allow it to be. As I mentioned before, stand your ground and stick to the plan. Once the seller realizes you're not going to play games, then counterpunch by sharing your data. Show them how you arrived at your equity and max bid figures, and especially all the various debt and risk attached to their home. Explain in detail how all the equity that's attracting investors is a perishable asset. Their bargaining position is shrinking every day and this is their last chance to get something out of the deal before it goes to auction.

If they're on the fence at this point and there's plenty of equity in the deal, you can even offer to sweeten the deal in a way no other cash investor will do. Offer them a provision in the side agreement for a small stake in the final sale, 1-3%, so they can profit from both ends of the deal. Obviously, this is a last resort, the last arrow in the quiver, but worth it before letting some big game slip away.

Property damage

Whether a recalcitrant home seller that's having second thoughts or a renter, the key to avoiding property damage isn't threats or intimidation. It's all about incentivizing them from the beginning to make them a partner. You can do this through contingent payouts to the homeowner or by adding extra cash into the security deposit for new tenants so they get "free" money if they leave the property in good condition.

While not everyone is perfectly reasonable, these simple strategies work the vast majority of the time. In the rare event a tenant is actively trying to blackmail you, don't get emotional. Go ahead and offer a little moving money. You always still have your writ of possession and can call the cops to drag them out, but if an extra few hundred bucks can avoid all these troubles, then why not? They're not getting the best of you, since you're still turning a generous profit. Sharing a smidgen to grease the wheels and keep everything moving smoothly is always preferable to getting petty revenge.

Stubborn lenders

We've talked a bit about the legal pressure you can unleash to bring irrational lenders to the bargaining table, and how you have the cost-effectiveness edge in that fight. It's also important to note that an investor has their own special leverage in these situations.

First off, the whole credit and life ruining foreclosure weapon, the "Sword of Damocles" they use to intimidate homeowners has no effect on you. They can either negotiate and get most of what they want, or sell the debt to a debt collector for pennies on the dollar. Either way, no skin off your back. You're really doing them a favor.

Second, the more equity in a deal, the more skin you have in the game, but the less they do. That might sound like leverage for them at first, until you think about the opportunity costs. The lender has less to gain from taking the foreclosure to auction, so they won't be willing to invest as much in attorney fees. Let alone for the lender's rep to spend too much of their own personal time fighting you. It's just not cost efficient for them, but it is for you.

If lenders need reminding of the strength of your position, then a carrot and stick approach is quite useful. At the same time your lawyer files the latest delaying motion, reach out personally to the lender's point of contact and try to figure out how you can simplify everyone's life. Get personal with the lender's rep. Many of these companies won't be traditional banks, but also real estate investors themselves. There are so many interesting ways you can add value for each other besides squabbling over a few percentage points in the settlement.

This is one of my favorite topics and I go into great detail about alternative negotiating strategies in my online courses.

Sellers taking advantage of tax pressure

At some point or another, you're going to want to take advantage of the IRS's generous 1031 exchange program. While this is a great way to defer taxes and accumulate wealth, there is one big operational downside. One that savvy sellers are going to try and use against you in the hope of strong-arming you into paying a premium price for their property.

To roll over your capital gains and avoid paying taxes, you have 45 days to identify a replacement investment and 180 days to close. That adds a stress level that can lead to you making elementary risk management mistakes. Afterall, you now have to weigh the potential cost of a sudden tax bill if you bail on a new investment against the potential loss of staying in the position. This also gives sellers leverage over you. Even if you refuse to budge on price, they'll try to tack on all sorts of ridiculous terms and conditions, knowing you'll grudgingly submit to them instead of cutting a fat check to the IRS.

This can occur even when dealing with distressed homeowners. All they have to do is have one quick conversation with a seller's agent or a lawyer and they'll realize they can extract all sorts of last-minute concessions from you.

Thankfully, there is a simple way around all this. You'll obviously want to double check everything with your attorney and accountant to make sure you comply with the law, but there are legal ways out of this predicament.

Just purchase the replacement property before closing on the first and resell it to yourself. Yes, this requires more capital and there's more details involved, but it's far superior to letting sellers have leverage over you. In the online courses, I dive into intricate detail about exchange strategies. Especially how to leverage rental income to exchange your portfolio for ever more valuable properties.

Types of Properties You Should Be Weary Of As A Flipper Or Renter

While finding off-market homes with built-in equity is the single most important key to success in this business, only buying property you can sell fast or rent out quickly is a close second. This last part is quite often overlooked, even by experienced investors, especially when they're drooling over a deal that's too good to be true. No matter how large the spread between the equity you're buying and the price you pay, that "killer deal" can bleed you dry if you haven't factored in your holding and opportunity costs. Remember, time is money; money that's either going into or coming out of your pocket every single day.

That's why relatively small and boring homes in a cookie-cutter subdivision sell so much faster and with higher ROI than luxury beachfront condos.

So here are five red flags that aren't necessarily deal breakers, but they do signal it's time to step back and reevaluate your estimated equity. If you purchase properties like the following, you can expect either higher rehab costs, larger holding costs or even need to discount the listing price to move them.

The Unique/Charming/Quirky Home "With Character"

I'm sure you've seen these ultra-customized homes designed to fit a particular person's taste... and rarely anyone else. To a certain extent, you'll run into this problem with nearly every home you're planning on flipping, since you're focusing on off-market properties that haven't been professionally staged.

But the real problem isn't shag carpets, walls shining in lime green or psychedelic tiling in the kitchen. These cosmetic issues can be fixed up fast and cheap. I'm talking about the much harder to change "quirks" that make the property itself standout from the neighborhood.

For example, while there's nothing wrong with building a newer Colonial style house in the middle of a subdivision full of older Tudor style homes, it's not an ideal investment property. Or if there's an odd easement or some other neighborhood feature that hides the home, and its curb appeal, from the street. Maybe you want your personal house to stand out from the pack, but not when you're trying to flip a place in a hurry. Since time costs more than money in this industry, you want properties that have mass appeal so you can attract the widest pool of buyers as fast as possible.

Even if you can attract interest fast, many of your prospects will still have trouble qualifying for their loans. The more your property differs from the nearby comps, the more appraisals, inspections and surveys the bank will order, all costing the buyer cash up front and tempting them to hunt for another house.

The Castle In A Village

Hand in hand with avoiding unique homes, you don't want to hold the biggest property in an area. The simple truth is the largest home in a neighborhood will have the smallest price per square foot. Generally speaking, you'd rather buy a home that's a bit smaller than average for the area, then let the sales prices of the neighbors lift up the value of your investment, rather than the other way around.

On top of that, rehabbing a larger home simply eats up more of your capital. Even modest renovations to a larger property will cost more in paint, fixtures, labor hours, etc. Costliest of all though, a bigger project will take more of your time to rehab. So buy those properties a bit smaller than the neighborhood's average size, place them on the market as soon as you get title and offload as fast as possible with the bare minimum investment in renovation. I know, this strategy of flipping average, boring homes is far from glamourous. No one is going to make a reality TV show about you, but this does guarantee you'll still be in business for years to come.

Old Timers

While turnover speed is your top concern and equity a close second, minimizing risk should always hover over every decision you make, like a nagging angel on your shoulder. And the simple truth is that the older a home, the more risk you're assuming, no matter how great a deal it is or how fast you think you can sell it. The older the house, the more likely you are to underestimate the repair and renovation costs, as well as the time required to fix things up. This all might seem obvious, but you'll be surprised how often investors get tunnel vision over the "great deal" they're about to land and glaze over the nitty gritty hurdles of flipping the property.

I mentioned earlier how one of the most common failures for flippers is not accurately estimating their total costs. A big part of what trips them up is when they're dealing with older houses, since there are so many hidden problems that can throw off your estimate. Even if there aren't any major age-related flaws, there's a good chance yours is not the home's first renovation. So when renovating someone else's renovation, you can always expect additional costs and delays to pop up. Still, we're always tempted to invest because these homes are usually quite cheap, often with the original mortgage paid off, and they include incredible equity built-in… but there's no such thing as a free lunch.

Sure, you can tell if the roof needs replacement, but can your home inspector say for sure that the older pipes aren't leaking somewhere? What about the gradual effects of settlement reaching critical mass somewhere? Why is there new flooring everywhere in this old house? What were the owner's covering up?

Even if construction and heavy renovations are your forte, you still have outdated styles to contend with. Which makes older homes usually not so popular with younger buyers. For example, these properties tend to have smaller bedrooms, closets, and bathrooms than more modern homes, not to mention rarely having the open or split

163

floor plans that are popular among buyers today. That's not to say no one will be interested, but since speed is top consideration, we need to stick with homes that have the widest appeal as possible.

While these homes might still be tempting, you're assuming much more risk than with a newer home. And as professional investors, we're always striving to minimize risk. So stack the odds in your favor and shy away from the old timer homes.

The Home With "Easy Access To Everything"

Does the home lay directly on a major thoroughfare? What's perfect for commercial property is scary for residential buyers. First off, you can count out most families with small children from even stopping by. I mean, would you let your own kids play in the front yard of a property just feet from a busy street while you're talking to prospects? How do you think other parents feel about living there?

Second, even for many other buyers without children, that "convenience" is an annoyance. Who wants trucks honking back and forth, ambulances and cop cars blaring sirens during the night or all the annoying folks using your driveway to back up because they missed their turn?

Since you're cutting out so much of the potential customer base just because of the location, you can expect these properties to take much longer to move. When these homes finally do sell, they go for much less than an identical house just a block away from the main road. So avoid these high traffic areas for both your own peace of mind and to minimize risk.

Any Home In A Neighborhood That Doesn't Radiate A Good Vibe

Now I'm not trying to run-down any community. There are always some great people and comfortable homes in even the worst parts of town. However, as an investor, you can't count on buyers respecting that nuance and recognizing the hidden charm of seemingly "bad"